WILD GAME COOKBOOK

A Remington Sportsmen's Library Book

WILD GAME COOKBOOK

EDITED BY
L. W. "BILL" JOHNSON, "THE HUNTER"

A BENJAMIN COMPANY/RUTLEDGE BOOK

NEW YORK, NEW YORK

Cover Photo: Robert Stahman

On the Cover: Roast Venison, Mallard Ducks in Grand Marnier Sauce, Rabbit Creole, Wild Game Ragout, Pheasant Epicure with Wild Rice. Quimper Dinnerware on the cover supplied by Foreign Advisory Service Corporation, 225 Fifth Avenue, New York City, sole importers.

ISBN 0-87502-907-8
Prepared and produced by Rutledge Books
Published by The Benjamin Company, Inc.
485 Madison Avenue, New York, New York 10022
Library of Congress Catalog Card Number 70-114972
Printed in the United States of America
Fourth Printing, September 1977
Special Printing for
PURINA® HIGH PROTEIN DOG MEAL®

CONTENTS

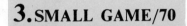

INTRODUCTION

Through the years, people have asked me when and where my interest in cooking started. I can tell you—at a very young age. My father was a great outdoorsman, and a good cook—and an excellent teacher. At the age of six, I was planning a camping trip. Dad looked over my supplies, found a custard pie I'd appropriated, some ham salad, eggs and bread. He said, "When you're going out in the woods, boy, take food that won't spoil and make you sick. With no doctor around, who knows what could happen." That shook me up a bit. He also taught me to keep my cooking utensils hospital clean, because they are another potential source of trouble.

So my father and I hunted and fished and cooked our game. I was the apprentice. From my dad I learned how to shoot rabbits, dress them, wash them up, season them, roll them in flour, add bacon grease, and fry them. We had meals that were fit for a king. We were never satisfied. We always tried something new. But always, the fire had to be just right: just coals—a blaze smokes up the meat.

My father taught me how to prepare a prairie chicken, or any bird we might take: clean it inside, season it inside, feathers still on, and wrap it in yellow clay mixed with water to make a paste, seal up the body cavity. Then open up the bed of coals, put the bird down in the bottom, cover it, leave it for a couple of hours. When you dig it up again, the clay will be as hard as a rock. When cracked carefully, feathers and skin come off, leaving nice clean, tasty meat.

Finally, cooking became a matter of competition between Dad and me. It was fun. I was a lucky boy.

Later, during the eighteen years I was doing exhibition and promotion work for Remington, covering the greater portion of the United States, I'd exchange recipes with Remington people and other hunters. I'd talk to old-timers and learn their secrets in preparing game. This led to quite an accumulation of recipes—some I've modified, added to, subtracted from.

One thing I learned from my grandmother, a pioneer in central Illinois. A good portion of their diet was game, so she knew. She said: "Never hurry it . . . always take plenty of time in cooking game. Cook it slow," she said. "Don't burn away all the flavor."

Many people today profess not to like wild game. "It's strong," they say. "It has a wild flavor." So it is very often wasted. This waste prompted me, several years ago, to contact Breta Griem who had a television show in Milwaukee, "What's New in the Kitchen." Once a month, for eight and a half years, I cooked game and fish on her program and outlined hunting hints. My sole reason was to get people to make the best use of game.

It's only a matter of knowing how. If your husband is a hunter, and you're both frustrated because you have never tried to cook wild game, but he likes to hunt . . . this book is *especially* for you. For game, if properly prepared, is excellent food. But proper care has to start in the field.

Dressing of Big Game: Speed is essential. Let's take the deer, for example. I do not recommend cutting the jugular vein. A deer's reflexes could cause the legs to thrash out and injure you. If you open the abdominal cavity, get all the entrails out, and hoist the deer off the ground so there's plenty of air circulation, you'll have done as much as you can. Take a 2- to 2 1/2-foot long stick, sharpen the ends, and spread the abdominal cavity open as wide as possible. That'll let more air in. When you get to camp, hang your deer by the head again, so it's off the ground. If the weather is warm, I suggest you get your deer to a locker or refrigerator plant as quickly as possible. If it's cold, there's no rush.

When hauling your deer home, don't lay it on the car's hood. The heat from the motor may start the meat spoiling.

At most locker plants, you can have your deer cut up whatever way you want. I think the hind legs make fine roasts. As for the neck meat and so-called trimmings, I take all the nice, clean, clear, meaty portions I can get boned out, and cut them up into chunks for hunter's stew or goulash. If you want some hamburger, you can grind them up yourself rather easily. When freezing, double-wrap your steaks and chops to protect them from freezer burn. As for thawing, don't rush it—do it slowly. But you can also roast or broil, boil or fry your meat while it's still cold. It just takes a little more time. Meat from the neck, front quarters and some of the rib sections that can't be cubed, can be ground and made into venison sausage.

Rabbits, Squirrels, and other small game: Here too, after the kill, dress the game quickly. Take your knife and brisk it back to the pelvis, open up the abdominal cavity, reach in, break the diaphragm, pull loose the heart, lungs and liver, and with a quick snap of the wrist, everything will come out. Remove the anal canal after splitting the pelvis, and your job's complete. If there's snow on the ground, grab a handful and pack the rabbit or squirrel with it for a few moments to take out excess blood, then snap it out. This will cool the animal and clean it. Some old-time hunters take off the head and four feet as well as entrails right on the spot . . . no sense carrying all that stuff home.

Now, as for freezing the game, my suggestion is to use a milk carton or a coffee can with a plastic lid, and pack your pieces of squirrel or rabbit in. Fill with water to about an inch from the top; it should cover all the meat.

I would like to add, stuff your small game animals with dried leaves, moss or grass or paper toweling when you're going to carry them in your hunting coat. The cleaning job won't be quite as hard when you get home.

To *start* that cleaning job, cut through the skin across the back an inch or so, so you can get two fingers from each hand in to pull the hide off. An old-timer once showed me how he stood on the tail and pulled the hide off.

Waterfowl: As with all other game taken in the field, to preserve the fine qualities of the bird or animal it's necessary to remove the entrails from the body and get it cooled as quickly as possible. If it isn't convenient to do this, as in duck hunting, for example, lay the birds out so the air can circulate around each one individually.

Any game taken with shotguns will have pellets penetrating the abdominal cavity and the intestines. The fluids from the intestines have a tremendous degenerative effect on body tissue, so the quicker you can remove the entrails from the bird and get it aired out and cooled, the better. In warm weather I would suggest with the larger birds, like wild geese, that as soon as you get the bird back to the blind, take your knife and cut the jugular vein, draw the bird, keep the vent open so air can circulate.

When you're cleaning your birds at home, fill a 12- or 14-quart pail with about 10 quarts of water. Bring to a boil and place about 3 pounds of paraffin in it and let it melt. While it's melting, remove the rough feathers from your birds. Dip the bird in the water and bring it back through the paraffin on top. Let this congeal, then dip again, two or three times. When the paraffin gets real hard, break and peel off, and the down and pin-feathers will come with it. Wash the bird in cold water, and it's ready for the oven or freezer.

Freeze in coffee cans as described before . . . or in plastic wrap. Be sure your birds are wet when you wrap them. The final wrapping is freezer paper, two layers. I do not recommend soaking the bird in vinegar water or soda or salt water. If anything, soak in cold water. Put some ice cubes in it. You might also take time to remove any pellets and blood clots. The proper care of game has so much to do with making it palatable!

Upland Game: Pheasants, ruffed grouse, prairie chicken, sharp-tail grouse, quail, Hungarian partridge, dove, turkey, chukar partridge and many other species all require the same treatment in the field. Dress them out as soon as possible, carry them on a game hanger so the air circulates around them. They'll come through much better than if you put them in an airtight canvas pocket. Birds stacked one upon the other have a tendency to heat up and spoil.

There's a debate among hunters as to whether our upland birds should be picked or skinned. Each person must decide for himself. However, pheasant, quail and Hungarian partridge can be scalded and wet-picked. Prairie chickens and sharp-tails can be scalded and picked. But some birds—ruffed grouse is one—have very thin and tender skin, which makes the job difficult. Some wild-game cooks insist the skin be left on, since fat is deposited just under it and that has a lot to do with imparting a more delicate flavor to the meat. Skinning a bird is rather simple. Start at the breast, peel the feathers off; cut off the legs at the knee joint. Take off the wings too. When the job's done, soak the bird in cold water. Prepare for eating or freezing in the manner described before.

To say, "I don't like any wild-game meat," is a pretty broad statement. It's like saying, "I don't like people." You haven't met them all. And so it is with game. Give it a chance—but be sure that, from the field to the pot, you've followed the accepted rules and suggested recipes. This could open up a whole new world of fine food for you.

Bill Johnson

UPLAND GAME BIRDS

Game birds offer the most varied—and perhaps the most delicious—wild meat. From the miniature woodcock up to the magnificent wild turkey, they provide a range of flavor as wide as the variation of sport in hunting them. The quality and flavor of game birds, however, depend to a great extent on the care they receive after the hunter has bagged them.

These are the simple rules to follow: The birds should be drawn soon after they are shot. Body heat should be allowed to dissipate as quickly as possible; the birds should be kept at cool—better still, cold—temperatures until they are cooked.

When testing game birds to identify those that are young and tender, the stiffness of the bill is a good guide. If pheasant and grouse, for example, can be lifted by the lower jaw without breaking it, they are mature birds whose jaws are set. They will not be as tender as the younger, less developed birds and will require longer cooking, perhaps moist cooking, such as braising.

Young pheasants' spurs will be pliable. The breast bone of a young partridge will break easily, and the leg will be plump close to the foot. The claws of a young bird of any kind are sharp—in an older bird, the claws are blunter at the tip. If the bird is old, a commercial tenderizer will be a help. Follow package directions, but use the tenderizer in the cavity, rather than on the outside of the bird.

Game birds should not be packed together in a mass if there is any warmth left in them or if the weather is mild. When in camp at a distance from any settlement, the birds should be allowed to air thoroughly each night or should remain hung in a cool, airy place until the trip is over. If a freezing locker is available, the birds should be cleaned and packaged separately in plastic film, heavy-duty foil, or other moisture-vaporproof wrapping.

The best methods of handling and preparing different types of game birds vary, and suggestions are made for each type under its special classification throughout the book. Although handling of birds may differ with the individual, according to his preference, only the best—and the safest—procedures for dealing with game of all sorts are covered in this book.

As for how many you can serve with your bag, that depends partly on the recipe—is the bird to be stuffed, braised with accompanying vegetables, cooked in a potpie? If so, a single bird will go farther. In general, however, a pheasant will serve three or four, a partridge one—or two if it's very large. With quail and woodcock, count on one bird for each serving.

In stuffing any kind of game bird, bear this in mind: Do not put the stuffing into the bird until the stuffing has cooled; in any case, do not stuff until a short time before the bird is to be cooked; if any time must elapse, refrigerate the bird immediately after stuffing and sewing or skewering.

GROUSE, PARTRIDGE, PRAIRIE CHICKEN

Skin or pluck the bird, as you prefer. Remove the head and cut off legs at middle joint. Remove entrails. Wipe the cavity with a cloth wrung out of cold water. For packing and shipping information, see page 168.

CASSEROLE OF PARTRIDGE

partridge breasts and legs
1 carrot, sliced
2 onions, sliced
3/4 pound mushrooms, sliced
1 can cream of mushroom soup
1/2 cup milk
1 large can chow mein noodles
salt, pepper

Parboil partridge breasts and legs with carrot, onion, in water to cover for about 30 minutes. Drain and take meat from bones. Mix together meat, mushrooms, mushroom soup diluted with milk, and noodles. Taste and season if necessary. Turn into well-buttered casserole. Bake in 350°F. oven 1 1/2 hours.

PARTRIDGE, HUNTER'S STYLE

4 partridge
salt, pepper
4 cups shredded cabbage
4 slices bacon cooked, crumbled
16 large cabbage leaves
2 tablespoons butter
1 cup chicken broth
4 carrots, sliced
1/4 teaspoon crushed thyme
1/4 teaspoon crushed tarragon
1 teaspoon salt
1/4 teaspoon pepper

Sprinkle partridge inside and out with salt and pepper. Combine shredded cabbage and bacon. Spoon one-fourth of the mixture into cavity of each bird. Wrap each with 4 cabbage leaves and fasten with string. Place in a large skillet; add butter, chicken broth, and remaining ingredients. Bring liquid to boil. Reduce heat, cover and simmer 25 to 30 minutes, or until tender. Remove string and cabbage leaves. Serve with sauce in pan. Serves 4.

PARTRIDGE BREASTS STROGANOFF

Sauté fine-diced onion in 2 tablespoons butter. Do not brown. Remove and reserve the onion, and place partridge breasts (with more butter, if needed) in the pan. Cook gently until tender. Remove from pan, keep warm in oven. In the same pan, brown 3/4 cup sliced mushrooms, adding salt and pepper and 1 teaspoon basil. Add the partridge breasts and cooked onion; stir in 3/4 cup sour cream. Heat, and serve on toast.

BREAST OF GROUSE, TOMATO SAUCE

2 grouse
salt, pepper
butter
1/2 cup diced celery
1/4 cup diced carrots
2 slices onion
2 sprigs parsley
1 bay leaf

Remove breasts from grouse, season with salt and pepper and saute in butter. Place the other pieces of grouse in saucepan, cover with cold water; add celery, carrots, onion, parsley and bay leaf. Cook until stock is reduced to 3/4 cup. Strain the stock and use in making Tomato Sauce (below). Arrange breast meat on serving dish and surround with sauce. Serves 4.

Tomato Sauce

3/4 cup stock
3 tablespoons butter
4 1/2 tablespoons flour
3/4 cup canned tomatoes
salt and cayenne pepper
1 tablespoon lemon juice
1 teaspoon finely chopped parsley
1/2 cup canned mushrooms, sliced

Thicken stock from grouse with butter and flour. Add tomatoes; season with salt, cayenne and lemon juice; add chopped parsley and sliced mushrooms.

GROUSE IN VELVET SAUCE

Put birds in dutch oven or pressure cooker. Add 1/4 teaspoon salt and a dash of pepper for each bird. Add 1 small whole onion, 2 celery stalk tops with leaves, and about 1 cup water. Simmer 1 1/2 to 2 hours or until tender, or pressure-cook 20 minutes at 15 pounds. Remove birds from liquid and cool. Break meat into small pieces. Stir into Velvet Sauce (below) and heat. Serve at once over toast.

Velvet Sauce

Melt 2 tablespoons butter over low heat. Stir in 2 tablespoons flour until well blended. Cook over low heat, stirring until mixture is smooth and bubbly. Remove from heat. Gradually stir in 1 chicken bouillon cube dissolved in 1 cup hot water. Bring to boil, stirring constantly, and boil for 1 minute. Add salt to taste and a dash of white pepper. This makes enough sauce for 1 bird.

This recipe serves equally well for partridge or quail.

SUGAR-SHACK PARTRIDGE

2 large partridge
1/3 cup flour
2 teaspoons paprika
1/3 cup butter
1 teaspoon salt
1/2 teaspoon pepper
1 cup water

Cut up birds, remove breast bone, discard kidney section. Coat pieces with flour and paprika. Brown slowly in butter. Season with salt and pepper. Add water and cook until tender, about 45 minutes, depending on age of bird. Transfer partridge to a 3-quart casserole. Add 1 can cream of chicken soup and 1 1/2 cans of milk to pan in which partridge was browned and bring to boil. Pour over meat in casserole. Tuck 2 onions, quartered, among pieces of meat. Top with 14 to 16 dumplings (below). Bake uncovered in 425°F. oven 25 minutes. Serve with extra gravy made of 1 can cream of chicken soup, 1/2 can milk, 1 cup sour cream. Mix and bring to a boil. Serves 6.

Sugar-Shack Dumplings

2 cups flour
4 teaspoons baking powder
1/2 teaspoon salt
1 teaspoon poultry seasoning
1 teaspoon celery seed
1 teaspoon onion flakes
1 tablespoon poppy seed
1/4 cup salad oil
1 cup milk
1/4 cup butter
2/3 cup crushed cracker crumbs

Sift together all dry ingredients except cracker crumbs. Add salad oil, milk; stir until moistened. Drop by tablespoon over casserole. Melt butter, add cracker crumbs. Sprinkle over tops of dumplings. Bake uncovered in 425°F. oven 25 minutes.

FOIL-BAKED PARTRIDGE

Clean bird. Salt and butter inside and out. Place 1 bay leaf in cavity. Lay several bacon strips over bird. Wrap in aluminum foil. Place on baking pan, bake in 500°F. oven 30 minutes.

For outdoor cooking, bake the Foil-baked Partridge covered with coals in campfire until tender, about 25 minutes.

GROUSE AND KRAUT

2 grouse, cleaned
bacon drippings OR butter
1 No. 3 can sauerkraut

Cut grouse in serving pieces. Brown well in hot bacon fat or butter. Remove meat, spread half of sauerkraut over bottom of skillet. Lay meat on this and cover with balance of the kraut. Cover skillet and simmer until meat is tender, about 2 hours, adding a little water as needed to prevent bottom layer from scorching. Serves 2 to 3.

CHAFING DISH BIRDS

1/2 dozen small partridge
6 small red peppers, fine-cut
salt, pepper
butter
1/2 cup stock OR hot water
2 tablespoons worcestershire sauce
juice of 1 lemon
2 cans small mushrooms
1 cup cream

Split birds open. Sprinkle with red peppers. Place in chafing dish breast down; season. On back of each bird place 1-inch square of butter; add stock or water. Cover dish and steam until butter is well melted. Mix worcestershire sauce and lemon juice, add to birds. Cook 1/2 hour; add mushrooms. When birds are tender, add cream. Serves 6.

BAKED PARTRIDGE BREAST

Clean and skin partridge, saving meaty breast only. Rinse well with water. Dip breast into flour seasoned with salt and pepper. Brown in hot fat. Place meat in roasting pan; pour over cream of chicken soup (allow 1 can soup diluted with 1/2 can water for 2 partridge). Bake covered in 325°F. oven 1 1/4 hours. Remove cover, bake 15 minutes longer to brown. Make gravy from pan drippings. Each partridge breast serves 1.

OYSTER-STUFFED GROUSE

1 cleaned grouse
1 cup breadcrumbs
salt, pepper
1/4 cup chopped celery
1/2 pint raw oysters
4 strips bacon

Brown breadcrumbs in butter, season with salt and pepper; add celery and oysters. Stuff the bird with this mixture. Fasten bacon strips across breast and roast covered in 425°F. oven 45 minutes, basting occasionally. Serves 1.

BRAISED PARTRIDGE

1 partridge
4 carrots, sliced
1 onion, sliced
flour
bacon OR salt pork drippings
thyme OR bay leaf
salt, pepper, paprika
spiced salt OR meat stock

Cut bird into pieces. Split breast. Dust partridge, carrots and onion with flour; sauté in deep pan in bacon or salt pork fat until bird is browned. Add seasoning and cover with water. Bake in 350°F. oven until meat is done—1 1/2 to 2 hours. Serve with gravy made from pan drippings. Serves 2.

BROILED GROUSE

4 grouse
1 large onion, halved
3 stalks celery
1/2 teaspoon salt
dash pepper
1/2 cup olive oil

Clean grouse; split down the back. Put in a deep pot and cover with water. Add onion, celery, salt and pepper. Cover and simmer 30 minutes. Remove birds from pan, drain. Brush with oil, then place skin side down on broiler rack. Broil 15 minutes or until brown, turning once and basting frequently with oil. Serves 4.

15

SMOTHERED GROUSE

Split grouse in half, roll in flour which has been seasoned with salt, pepper and thyme. Brown in hot butter, along with mushroom caps. When all is delicately browned, pour over enough heated heavy cream to half cover the birds. Cover tightly and bake in 350°F. oven until birds are tender—about 1/2 hour for older birds. Serve with sauce from pan.

PARTRIDGE AND DUMPLINGS

2 or 3 partridge breasts
salt, pepper
flour
butter
2 cans cream of mushroom soup
1 egg
1/2 cup milk
2 cups packaged biscuit mix
1/2 cup wild rice, cooked
2 3-ounce cans sliced mushrooms
(optional)

Salt and pepper breasts, roll in flour and brown in butter. Place in roasting pan and add 1 can of cream of mushroom soup, thinned with 1/2 can water. Bake in 350°F oven 3 hours. For dumplings, mix egg with milk, add biscuit mix. Stir in cooked wild rice. Pour juice from roasted breasts into an electric frying pan. Add 1 can cream of mushroom soup and 2 cans of water. Bring to boil. Drop on dumpling mix by tablespoonfuls, cook for 20 minutes with vent open. Serve mushroom gravy from frying pan over the partridge breasts and dumplings. Garnish with steaming hot mushroom slices. Serves 2 or 3.

GROUSE WITH ORANGE SLICES

4 grouse
salt, pepper
4 1/4-inch-thick orange slices,
peeled and seeded
4 slices bacon
1/4 cup butter, melted
grated rind 1 orange
2 tablespoons orange juice
1 teaspoon lemon juice
chopped parsley

Sprinkle grouse inside and out with salt and pepper. Cover breast of each with an orange slice and a bacon slice; fasten with string. Place grouse breasts up in a baking pan. Roast in preheated 350°F. oven 15 to 20 minutes, or until tender, basting frequently with combined butter, orange rind and juice and lemon juice. Remove string. Sprinkle with parsley. Serve with the roasted orange and bacon slices. Serves 4.

Baked hominy and baby brussels sprouts go well with these delicious grouse.

RUFFED GROUSE AMANDINE

4 ruffed grouse
salt, pepper
4 slices bacon
1/2 cup butter, melted
1/4 cup blanched almonds, slivered
1 teaspoon lemon juice
4 slices buttered toast

Sprinkle grouse inside and out with salt and pepper. Cover breasts with bacon and fasten with string or wooden picks. Place grouse breasts up in baking pan. Roast in preheated 350°F. oven 15 to 20 minutes, or until tender, basting frequently with 1/4 cup of the butter. Combine remaining butter, almonds and lemon juice. Five minutes before grouse are done, remove string or picks and bacon. Pour butter-almond mixture over grouse. Serve on buttered toast with bacon, buttered peas, endive salad and ale or beer. Serves 4.

PARTRIDGE IN HALF-AND-HALF

Brown cut partridge pieces dredged in flour. When browned place in deep skillet or dutch oven and add 1 pint of half-and-half (half beer, half ale). Simmer until half-and-half is absorbed. Gradually add 1/2 to 1 cup boiling water. Continue simmering until tender. Season to taste.

PARTRIDGE IN WINE SAUCE

3 whole partridge breasts
1 onion, thin-sliced
1 tablespoon chopped celery
1/4 teaspoon dried tarragon
1/2 cup white wine
4 tablespoons butter
3 tablespoons flour
1/2 teaspoon salt
dash pepper
2 tablespoons butter
1 egg yolk, slightly beaten
3 tablespoons heavy cream

Cut breasts in half along breastbone. Pull off skins. Place breasts, onion, celery, tarragon and wine in large saucepan. Add just enough boiling water to cover breasts. Cover; simmer 30 minutes or until partridge is tender. Remove breasts and keep warm. Strain liquid, boil to reduce to 2 cups. Melt the 4 tablespoons butter; stir in flour, salt and pepper. Gradually add the 2 cups partridge broth. Cook, stirring constantly, until mixture is smooth and thickened; add the 2 tablespoons butter and simmer gently 5 minutes, stirring occasionally. Combine egg yolk and cream; stir into hot sauce. Serve breasts covered with sauce. Serves 3.

Serve this on toast points or small squares of puff paste for a delicious gourmet touch.

CREAMED RUFFED GROUSE OR PARTRIDGE

3 to 4 grouse, skinned and cleaned
2 to 3 tablespoons butter
1 tablespoon salt
1/4 teaspoon pepper

Melt butter in 4- to 6-quart pressure cooker and brown birds. Add 1/2 cup water. Cover pressure cooker and cook for 15 to 20 minutes, or until tender and meat comes off bone. Season. Remove birds; take meat from bones. To make gravy, heat 2 cups broth from cooker (if not enough broth add water), with 1 cup sweet cream. Add 2 tablespoons cornstarch dissolved in cold water, stir until thickened. Reheat meat in gravy. Serve with whipped potatoes, rice or noodles. Serves 4.

BARBECUED PARTRIDGE

4 or 5 partridge
1 14-ounce bottle catsup
3 teaspoons salt
1/2 cup onion, chopped
1/2 cup sweet pickle relish
3 cups brown sugar

Place partridge in casserole or baking dish. Mix together remaining ingredients and pour over birds. Bake in 375°F. oven 3 hours, turning occasionally to brown evenly.

PARTRIDGE SUPREME

1 or 2 partridge, cut in serving pieces
3 tablespoons butter
1 teaspoon seasoned salt
1 can cream of chicken OR
mushroom soup
1/2 medium onion, diced

Fry partridge pieces in butter until golden brown, about 10 minutes for each side. Sprinkle with seasoned salt. Place in casserole and add soup and diced onion. Cover; bake in 350°F. oven 1 hour.

Delicious when served with rice or your favorite potatoes.

GROUSE OR SAGE HEN WITH RICE CREOLE

2 grouse, cut in serving pieces
3 stalks celery, cut in small pieces
1 tablespoon minced parsley
2 teaspoons salt
2 bay leaves
1/8 teaspoon garlic powder
2 dashes cayenne pepper
4 cups water
2 cups rice
1 package frozen peas and carrots,
cooked

Brown grouse lightly in butter. Add all ingredients except rice and carrots and peas. Simmer 3 to 4 hours, or until meat will come easily off bones. Cut meat into small pieces. Use 4 cups grouse broth to cook rice; bring to boil, reduce heat, cover, then simmer 15 minutes, or until broth is absorbed. When rice is nearly done, add grouse, and peas and carrots; heat all together for the last 3 or 4 minutes of cooking time.

You may also use one 3 1/2 pound sage hen in this recipe with excellent results.

POT ROAST OF GROUSE, PHEASANT OR QUAIL

2 grouse
2 tablespoons butter
3 tablespoons flour
1/2 teaspoon salt
2 cups water
1/4 cup black currant jelly

Clean birds well, dry thoroughly. Heat butter in frying pan; add birds, browning well on all sides. Combine flour and salt and rub mixture well on the outside of each bird. Arrange birds breast up in pan. Add 1/2 cup of water, heat to boiling, then turn heat down to low so mixture barely simmers. Add water at 15-minute intervals, as needed. Cook 45 minutes to 1 hour, or until tender. Then stir jelly into drippings in pan and serve sauce separately. Serves 2.

This recipe is equally good using 1 pheasant or 4 quail.

PARTRIDGE OR PHEASANT PIE

Early in the day, simmer 2 partridge or 1 pheasant in water to cover, to which 1 1/2 teaspoons salt and 1/4 teaspoon pepper have been added, until meat can be removed easily from bones. Remove birds from broth to cool. Use broth to cook till nearly tender:

2 large stalks celery, thin-sliced
1/4 green pepper, fine-chopped
1 medium onion, thin-sliced
1 carrot, thin-sliced
2 large potatoes, diced

Meantime, make biscuit dough as follows: Mix 2 cups flour with 1 teaspoon salt, 4 teaspoons baking powder. Cut in 5 to 7 tablespoons shortening. Add milk, and gently mix just enough to handle; pat and roll to fit the top of a baking bowl.

Drain the cooked vegetables, and make a thin gravy with the broth, adding 1 teaspoon salt, 1 teaspoon poultry seasoning OR ground sage, flour-and-water thickening. Place drained vegetables evenly over bottom of baking pan. Arrange meat in bite-size pieces over the vegetables. Cover with gravy, and top with biscuit dough. Cut several slits to allow steam to escape. Bake in 375°F. oven until biscuit is nicely browned —35 to 45 minutes. Serve with the remaining gravy. Serves 4 to 5.

RUFFED GROUSE AND WILD RICE

16 pieces grouse (raw)
2 cans cream of celery soup
2 cans cream of chicken soup
1 can drained mushrooms
2 cans water
1 package dry onion soup mix
1 cup wild rice washed, soaked
in hot water
1 cup white rice

Mix all ingredients except grouse in 9- x 13-inch baking pan. Lay grouse pieces on top of mixture. Salt grouse. Bake, covered with foil, in 350°F. oven 1 hour. Uncover, continue baking about 1/2 hour or until rice is cooked. Serves 6.

This dish may be made equally well using all wild rice instead of half white rice.

SAUTÉED PARTRIDGE SLICES

1 partridge breast
1 cup flour
1/2 teaspoon paprika
salt, pepper
1 tablespoon butter

Throughly clean partridge breast, remove skin. Cut into thin slices. Dip each slice of meat in mixture of flour, paprika, salt and pepper. Preheat a heavy skillet, preferably cast iron. Slowly sauté breast slices in butter over low heat until crisp and golden brown, about 12 or 15 minutes on each side. Serves 1 to 2.

This rich white meat is especially enjoyable served with a tossed salad, buttered vegetables, baked potatoes, French bread, warm apple pie, and hot coffee.

CARAMEL GROUSE

breasts and legs of grouse
2 quarts boiling water
1 onion, fine-diced
2 stalks celery, diced
1 tablespoon salt
dash pepper
Caramel Sauce

Place the meat, water, onion, celery, salt and pepper in a large kettle and simmer until tender, about 1 1/2 hours. Then remove the meat, in small pieces, from the bones and simmer in Caramel Sauce (below) about 1/2 hour.

Caramel Sauce

1/4 cup butter
1 cup brown sugar (firmly packed)
2 tablespoons water
2 tablespoons maple-flavored syrup

Melt butter in heavy skillet; then add sugar, water and syrup and stir to blend well. Add meat; simmer. Enough for 2 grouse.

WILD GROUSE DELUXE

3 grouse, cleaned, cut in serving
pieces
1 egg, slightly beaten
1/2 cup milk
1 teaspoon each: salt, pepper
garlic salt to taste
1 cup flour
1/4 cup butter
1/2 cup vegetable oil
1 can golden mushroom soup
1 cup water

Dip pieces of grouse in mixture of egg, milk, salt, pepper, garlic salt; then roll pieces in flour. Put butter and oil in skillet and heat to frying temperature. Brown pieces well on all sides. Remove from skillet and place in a single layer in cake pan. Add drippings from skillet to mushroom soup and mix well. Spoon over pieces of grouse. Add water to bottom of cake pan. Cover with aluminum foil and bake in 350°F. oven 1 hour, or until tender. Serves 4 to 6.

Grouse makes a tasty meal; with this recipe, the result is a desirably moist bird.

FRUIT-STUFFED PARTRIDGE

Clean partridge as quickly as possible after shooting. Soak in several changes of cold water 1 hour. Freeze or refrigerate until ready to cook. Rub inside of partridge with salt and pepper, then stuff cavity of bird with: 4 to 6 pieces of pineapple chunks, 4 to 6 pitted prunes, 4 to 6 apricot halves, 4 tablespoons butter, and juice of 1/2 orange. Brush outside of bird with soft butter, season with salt and pepper. Wrap bird tightly in heavy-duty aluminum foil. Place in roasting pan, breast side up, and bake in 350°F. oven 2 to 2 1/2 hours. Open foil and pour off drippings; thicken for gravy. Fold foil away from breast and brush generously with soft butter and return to oven for 15 to 20 minutes to brown.

PARTRIDGE AU VIN

partridge
port or sherry wine
6 cloves
3 slices onion
1 piece of bay leaf
1 teaspoon sage

Cut the birds into serving pieces. Place in a bowl with wine to cover. Add remaining ingredients. Cover and let stand in a cool place for 2 days. Drain the birds, reserving the liquid. Wipe dry and dip in flour. Brown in a small amount of shortening. Put birds and liquid into a casserole. Cover and bake in 300°F. oven 1 to 1 1/2 hours or until tender. Remove birds. Strain the liquid and boil rapidly about 15 minutes or until reduced by half. Thicken if desired and serve with the partridge.

This recipe works equally well with pheasant or grouse.

LARDED GROUSE

Lay thin slices of bacon on each bird until bird is completely covered. Wrap with twine to keep bacon in place. Put in roasting pan and pour sufficient water over birds to provide basting liquid. Cook in 400°F. oven 20 to 25 minutes. When done, remove strips of bacon, brush birds with melted butter, dredge with flour, and place in the oven until birds turn rich brown. Thicken liquid in pan, season, and add 1/2 cup of port or sherry to make gravy. Arrange birds on platter, garnish with rings of green peppers and the strips of bacon used to cover the birds while roasting.

ROASTED PRAIRIE CHICKEN

Wash chicken carefully; pat dry with paper towel. Stuff cavity with celery leaves and 1/2 apple. Truss into shape. Roast in 425°F. oven 30 to 40 minutes. Baste frequently with melted butter or margarine. Remove stuffing before serving. Serves 2 to 3.

SCALLOPED PRAIRIE CHICKEN

1 prairie chicken
2 teaspoons vegetable oil
1 tablespoon cornstarch
1 cup milk
1 cup rich cream
1 teaspoon salt
1/4 teaspoon pepper
1 pint fresh breadcrumbs
1/2 can sliced mushrooms
melted butter

Boil chicken whole in salted water until very tender. Cool. Pull off skin. Cut meat, light and dark, into small pieces, making about a pint. Heat vegetable oil in saucepan; add cornstarch, stirring constantly to prevent burning. Add milk gradually, cook 5 minutes. Add cream, salt and pepper. Butter a baking dish. Put in a layer of sauce, then a layer of breadcrumbs, then chicken, then mushrooms, continuing layers until all are used. Add remaining sauce last. Cover top with 1/2 cup breadcrumbs moistened with melted butter. Bake in 400°F. oven until a rich brown, about 20 minutes. Serves 4.

FRIED PRAIRIE CHICKEN

1 prairie chicken, cut in serving
pieces
salt, pepper
flour
4 tablespoons butter

Plunge prairie chicken pieces into cold water; drain thoroughly, but do not wipe dry. Season with salt and pepper and dredge thickly with flour. Cook chicken slowly in hot butter. When chicken is brown and tender, about 45 minutes, remove to a hot platter. Make Cream Gravy (below) and serve with prairie chicken. Serves 4.

Cream Gravy

2 tablespoons butter
2 tablespoons flour
1/2 teaspoon salt
1/8 teaspoon pepper
1 cup milk
drippings from prairie chicken

Melt butter and blend in flour, salt and pepper. Add milk gradually, stirring constantly. Add drippings from prairie chicken and cook 2 to 3 minutes longer.

WILD TURKEY

Those who have had the pleasure of tasting them consider wild turkey the most delicious of all game birds. They should be plucked and then the down singed off in a flame. Remove the head and entrails and cut off the lower part of the legs at the middle joint. Wipe clean with a hot cloth.

CHESTNUT-STUFFED WILD TURKEY

1 wild turkey, 8 to 10 pounds
salt, pepper
1/2 pound sausage meat
1/2 cup chopped onion
1 cup chopped celery
1 teaspoon salt
1/4 teaspoon pepper
1/8 teaspoon crushed thyme
5 juniper berries, crushed
1/4 cup chopped parsley
1 cup cooked chestnuts, chopped
8 cups soft breadcrumbs (made of day-old bread)
4 to 6 slices bacon
melted bacon fat

Sprinkle turkey inside and out with salt and pepper. Cook sausage meat in skillet until well done. Add onion and celery; continue to cook until vegetables are tender. Add seasonings, chestnuts and breadcrumbs; mix well. Spoon stuffing lightly into neck and body cavities. Close openings with skewers and string. Cover breast with bacon slices and cheesecloth soaked in melted bacon fat. Pull legs upward, wild turkey fashion, and tie together with string. Turn wings under. Place turkey breast up on rack in roasting pan. Roast in preheated 325°F. oven 20 to 25 minutes per pound, or until tender, basting frequently. Remove cheesecloth, skewers and string. Serves 8.

SPANISH WILD TURKEY

1 cup cooked turkey, minced
1/4 cup minced ham
1 cup mashed potatoes
1/2 cup turkey gravy
salt, pepper
2 cups hot cooked rice
1 clove garlic, finely minced
3 pimientos, chopped fine
1/4 cup grated cheese

Mix meat and potatoes with gravy and season to taste. Put into 6 buttered ramekins and cover with layer of rice into which garlic and pimientos have been stirred. Sprinkle with cheese. Place in a 400°F. oven for 15 minutes, or until heated through. Serves 4.

YUM YUM WILD TURKEY

1 15-pound wild turkey
bacon fat
salt, pepper
1 cup chopped onion
2 cups chopped celery
1 1/2 cups white wine
1 muslin cloth (about 16 inches square)

Wash and dry turkey. Brush with bacon fat. Salt and pepper. Mix onion, celery, and 1 cup of white wine. Stuff bird with this mixture. Place turkey in shallow pan. Dip cloth in bacon fat and cover turkey with it. Roast in 300°F. oven 3 hours, basting often with drippings in pan and the remaining wine. If turkey varies in size from recipe, allow at least 20 to 25 minutes per pound roasting time. Before serving, discard onion and celery stuffing. Serves 8 to 10.

ROAST WILD TURKEY

1 wild turkey, 10 to 12 pounds
salt, pepper
1 onion, chopped
1 pound pork sausage
1 1/2 quarts soft breadcrumbs
1/4 teaspoon pepper
2 teaspoons salt
3 tablespoons parsley, chopped
bacon or melted bacon fat

Dress turkey, season with salt and pepper inside and out and weigh to determine cooking time— 20 to 25 minutes per pound. Make stuffing: Cook onion with sausage in skillet for 5 minutes; then add remaining ingredients except bacon. Moisten with a little hot water if too dry. Place turkey breast down in uncovered pan, stuff, and roast for half the total required time. Then turn bird breast up. Lay strips of bacon over breast or cover with piece of cloth dipped in bacon fat. Finish roasting. If cloth is used, remove it toward the last if a deeper brown is desired. Test by pushing sharp-tined fork into a thigh and the thick part of the breast. If fork enters easily and if juice has no red tint, the bird is ready. Serves 6 to 8.

BRAISED WILD TURKEY

1 wild turkey
salt, pepper
1 pound salt pork, sliced
1 quart consommé
1 onion, sliced
1 carrot, sliced
2 to 3 sprigs parsley
1 large stalk celery, chopped
1 bay leaf
pinch of thyme

Wash, drain and pat turkey dry. Season cavity with salt, pepper; stuff with half the salt pork slices, cover turkey with the rest. It may be necessary to secure the salt pork strips with toothpicks. Brown in 400°F. oven about 1 hour. Combine consommé, onion, carrot, parsley, celery, bay leaf and thyme. Remove salt pork and discard. Add consommé to turkey and cover tightly. Bake in 300°F. oven for 2 to 3 hours or until tender. Baste frequently with consommé mixture.

WOODCOCK

Woodcock are small migratory game birds of delicious flavor. They should be cleaned soon after being shot. For further handling information, see shipping instructions on page 168.

BROILED WOODCOCK

4 woodcock
salt, pepper
4 slices bacon
1/4 cup butter, melted
1 tablespoon chopped parsley
4 slices buttered toast

Sprinkle woodcock inside and out with salt and pepper. Wrap each with a slice of bacon and fasten with string or a wooden pick. Place woodcock in broiler pan about 6 inches from heat. Broil 8 to 10 minutes on each side, or until tender, basting frequently with butter. Remove string or wooden pick. Sprinkle with parsley. Serve on buttered toast. Serves 4.

LINGONBERRY-STUFFED WOODCOCK

In a small saucepan combine: 1 cup dry white wine, 1 scallion, 1 stalk celery, both minced, 2 pinches chervil, a pinch of tarragon. Simmer the mixture, covered, over low heat for 10 minutes. Strain the liquor and reserve. Clean 6 woodcock and rub inside with salt and pepper. Combine in a large bowl: 3/4 cup breadcrumbs browned in butter, 1/2 cup preserved lingonberries, 1 ounce cognac or brandy. Stir mixture gently and stir in 2 tablespoons heavy cream and dry white wine or enough to give stuffing good consistency. Stuff birds with mixture and sew them up. Roll birds in 2 tablespoons melted butter until they are well coated. Place in a small roasting pan. Roast in 400°F. oven 5 minutes, then reduce heat to 300°F. and roast 25 minutes or until tender. Baste alternately with reserve liquor and melted butter and pan juices. Transfer birds to heated platter. Put roasting pan over low heat, put in 1 scant cup heavy cream; stir until thickened and smooth, scraping up brown bits that cling to pan. Pour sauce over woodcock. Serves 6.

WOODCOCK IN WINE

2 woodcock
1 cup water
3 cups dry red wine
1 teaspoon salt
2 medium onions
4 whole black peppers
3 whole allspice
1 bay leaf
1 carrot
1 small bunch parsley
1 celery stalk
1 slice lemon rind
2 or 3 slices bacon
lemon juice
2 tablespoons butter
1 cup sour cream

Clean meat well and put in deep bowl. Bring to a boil the water, wine, salt, onions, spices, carrot, parsley, celery and lemon rind.

Pour hot mixture over meat. Cover well. Cool, then place in refrigerator for 5 days. Turn the meat every day. When ready to cook, remove meat from brine. With a sharp knife, make 2 or 3 slits in skin over the breast and insert bacon strips into slits. Brush with lemon juice. Fasten skin back in place with meat skewers. Heat butter in deep pan and add meat. Add all of the pickling mixture, and simmer until meat is almost tender. Remove the meat, and force the vegetables through a coarse strainer. Mix vegetables with 1 cup sour cream and add to meat. Roast in 325°F. oven until tender, basting often. Serve with dumplings. Serves 3.

To accompany these birds, serve an orange-and-onion salad.

BAKED WOODCOCK

Split birds into serving pieces, dip in milk, and dredge with flour. Fry until brown. Salt and pepper. Place in casserole, cover with cream (sweet or sour), and bake in 350°F. oven until tender.

ROAST WOODCOCK

Wash and wipe the birds and season lightly with salt and pepper, dredge with flour. Bake in 350°F. oven about 30 minutes. Serve them up on buttered toast, garnished with sliced oranges or orange jelly.

QUAIL

Quail may be either plucked or skinned. Most dyed-in-the-wool quail hunters maintain that it is worth the trouble it takes to pick off the feathers and singe off the remaining down in order to conserve the extra bit of flavor and moisture the skin affords. When the birds have been picked—or skinned —remove heads and cut off legs at the first joint above the foot. Cut open down the back in line with the backbone and draw out the entrails. Wipe the cavity clean with a cloth wrung out of hot water. For information on packing and shipping, see page 168.

BRAISED QUAIL

You may either pluck or skin quail. Wipe cavity clean with a damp cloth. Split quail. Roll in a mixture of flour and cornmeal. Have 4 tablespoons fat very hot in a dutch oven. Brown birds quickly on both sides. Then add a little water and turn heat low. Simmer an hour.

QUAIL WITH GRAPES AND HAZELNUTS

4 quail
salt, pepper, flour
1/4 cup butter
1/2 cup water
1/2 cup seedless grapes
2 tablespoons chopped hazelnuts
1 tablespoon lemon juice
4 buttered toast slices

Sprinkle quail inside and out with salt, pepper and flour. Melt butter in skillet; add quail and brown on all sides. Add water, cover and cook over low heat 15 minutes, or until tender. Add grapes and cook 3 minutes longer. Stir in nuts, lemon juice. Serves 4.

QUAIL BAKED IN WINE

6 quail, cleaned and trussed
1/2 cup fat
2 small onions, minced
2 whole cloves
1 teaspoon peppercorns
2 cloves garlic, minced
1/2 bay leaf
2 cups white wine
1/2 teaspoon salt
1/4 teaspoon pepper
few grains cayenne pepper
1 teaspoon minced chives
2 cups cream OR evaporated milk

Melt fat, add onions, cloves, peppercorns, garlic, and bay leaf, cook several minutes. Add quail and brown on all sides. Add wine, salt, pepper, cayenne and chives and simmer until tender, about 30 minutes. Remove quail to hot serving dish. Strain sauce, add cream and heat to boiling point. Pour over quail. Serves 6.

QUAIL A LA RENNERT

Clean birds thoroughly, but do not split. For each bird, sauté 1/4 pound bulk sausage; add an equal amount of breadcrumbs and stuff bird with this mixture. Rub birds with olive oil and dust with salt and pepper. Roast in 325°F. oven.

ROAST QUAIL IN GRAPE LEAVES

Dress and wash 2 quail, dust with salt. Stuff with the following:

6 small shallots, sliced
2 tablespoons vegetable oil
1/2 pound fresh mushrooms, chopped
2 tablespoons sherry
salt, pepper
1 tablespoon chopped parsley
1/2 cup breadcrumbs

Sauté the shallots in vegetable oil until a light golden brown. Add the mushrooms and sherry. Simmer until the liquid has reduced by half. Remove from heat and season with salt and pepper to taste. Add parsley and bread crumbs. Allow to cool, then stuff quail. Cover quail with a large grape leaf, place 2 slices bacon over leaf and tie around quail with string. Roast in 350°F. oven until tender. You may substitute a small can of mushrooms for the fresh ones. Serves 2.

QUAIL IN CASSEROLE

4 quail
salt
1/3 cup salad oil
1 carrot, finely chopped
1 small onion, minced
1 tablespoon minced green pepper
3/4 cup sliced fresh OR canned mushrooms
2 tablespoons flour
2 cups stock OR 4 bouillon cubes dissolved in 2 cups boiling water
1/3 cup white wine

Rub the whole birds lightly with salt, then brown in oil (or in part oil and part butter). Remove to heated casserole. In the same oil, sauté carrot, onion, green pepper, and mushrooms slowly about 5 minutes. Blend in flour, then gradually stir in heated stock. Season to taste with salt; pour this sauce and wine over quail. Cover and bake in 350°F. oven about 1 hour, or until birds are tender. Serves 4.

BRUNCH QUAIL

4 quail
salt, pepper, flour
1/4 cup butter
1/2 cup water
6 small mushrooms, sliced
2 tablespoons chopped parsley
4 buttered toast slices OR trenchers

Sprinkle quail inside and out with salt, pepper and flour. Melt butter in a skillet; add quail and brown on all sides. Add water and mushrooms. Cover and cook over low heat 10 minutes. Add parsley, cover, and cook 10 minutes longer, or until tender. Serve on Trenchers (below) with mushroom sauce in pan. Serves 4.

Trenchers

Cut french bread into 2-inch-thick slices or soft or hard rolls into halves, selecting bread or rolls slightly larger in size than a quail. Scoop center from each to make cup to hold bird. Butter and toast lightly.

Fried hominy squares and applesauce make this a meal to remember.

BARBECUED QUAIL

2 quail
1 pound butter
1 cup catsup OR chili sauce
1 cup vinegar
juice of 4 lemons
4 teaspoons worcestershire sauce
1 teaspoon meat extract
cayenne pepper, salt

Lay birds on wire rack placed over a pit in which hardwood, oak, or charcoal has burned down to red coals. Turn constantly until they are lightly browned. Melt butter in large pan; add other ingredients. Let simmer over fire few minutes. With long-handled fork remove birds from fire; dip in sauce and return to fire. Continue this process until birds are done. Place in steamer. Pour remainder of sauce over birds. Keep hot until ready to serve, turning occasionally in sauce. Serves 2.

QUAIL PIE

1 dozen quail
salt, pepper
1 onion, chopped fine
1 small bunch parsley, minced
3 whole cloves
1/2 pound salt pork, diced, browned
2 tablespoons browned flour
3 tablespoons butter
2 cups diced cooked potatoes
pie crust made with 3 cups flour

Clean well and split a dozen small birds or, if larger ones are included, cut into pieces of similar size. Place in large pot with 2 quarts water. Bring to boil. Skim off foam. Add salt and pepper, onion, parsley and cloves. Then add salt pork. Be sure water is deep enough to cover birds. Simmer until birds are fork tender. Thicken with browned flour, and simmer a few minutes. Stir in butter. Remove from heat and allow to cool. Have potatoes ready. Line sides of a large buttered baking dish with pie crust. Layer in birds and potatoes, alternating until dish is full. Pour on gravy and put on top crust. Bake in 375°F. oven until crust is done. Serves 12 to 14.

QUAIL WITH MUSHROOMS

Pick, draw, and singe birds. Wipe carefully, inside and out. Then bind each bird with a slice of bacon. Put birds into a buttered pan and baste occasionally while they are roasting. If large birds, they'll require about 1/2 hour to cook. When done, put them into warmer for 2 minutes, while you add 1 tablespoonful butter, a little hot water, and the juice of half a lemon to fat in the pan, stirring meanwhile to make gravy. Serve birds on toast with gravy poured over them. Garnish with wedge of lemon, currant or grape jelly or a favorite game sauce.

DUTCH-OVEN QUAIL

Roll quail in mixture of flour and cornmeal. Then brown birds quickly on both sides in moderate amount of fat piping hot in dutch oven. Add a little water and turn fire low to let simmer 1 hour. Season.

SOUTHERN-FRIED QUAIL

Dry pick quail, clean and wipe thoroughly, salt and pepper, and dredge with flour. Have a heavy deep-fry skillet ready with close-fitting cover 1/2 full of hot fat. Cook quail in fat a few minutes over hot fire. Then cover frying pan and reduce heat. Cook slowly until tender, turning quail to other side when golden brown. Serve on hot platter, garnished with thin slices of lemon and sprigs of parsley.

QUAIL WITH BLUEBERRIES

8 quail
salt, pepper
oil
lemon juice
4 cups blueberries
sugar
butter
bay leaves

Season quail with salt and pepper

inside and out. Rub generously with oil and lemon juice mixed in equal parts, inside and out. Stuff quail with blueberries, add 1/2 teaspoon sugar after filling cavity. Hold cavity closed at rear by skewers or sew with cotton thread. Wrap each quail loosely in aluminum foil which must be folded well to keep in juices. Add 1 tablespoon butter and bay leaves before closing. Roast, breast down, in 425°F. oven 1 hour. Save juice and pour over hot platter. Serves 4.

BROILED QUAIL

Carefully wash dressed quail. Pat dry with absorbent paper. Wrap thin strip of bacon around each quail. Broil under hot flame 8 to 10 minutes. Serve with lemon-butter sauce if desired.

PIGEONS, DOVES

Handle pigeons and doves as you would any other game bird. The meat of pigeons is dark, with an excellent flavor. However, pigeon is not always tender and is best cooked by some slow, moist method, such as braising. Doves, smaller in size, also have dark meat, but are more tender. Unless very small, one dove or one pigeon serves one person.

DOVE BREASTS STROGANOFF

12 to 18 dove breasts
1 medium onion
1 can cream of celery soup
1 can mushrooms
1/2 cup sauterne
oregano
rosemary
salt, pepper
Kitchen Bouquet (for color)
1 cup sour cream

Place meat in a large baking dish; do not crowd. Dice and sauté onion; mix with remaining ingredients except sour cream. Pour over meat. Cover lightly with foil. Bake in 325°F. oven for 1 hour, turning occasionally. Add sour cream, stir. Bake uncovered 20 minutes. Serve over combined white and wild rice. Serves 6 to 8.

You can add the rice to the dove breast, and make a casserole.

BRAISED DOVES

6 dove breasts
salt, pepper
flour
cooking fat

Coat doves with seasoned flour by shaking flour and dove breasts in a bag. Brown on all sides in fat. Remove breasts. Leave 3 tablespoons fat in skillet. Sift in about

31

2 tablespoons flour and brown, stirring. Stir in salt, pepper and water to make gravy. Place browned doves in gravy and cook over low heat until tender. Serves 3 to 4.

DOVES IN WINE SAUCE

In a double-boiler top or a small heavy saucepan, melt 4 tablespoons butter; stir in 4 tablespoons flour. Blend well over low heat. Stir in 2 cups cold milk or milk and cream. To keep sauce smooth, use blending fork or wire whisk. Bring slowly to boiling point. Cook 2 minutes, stirring constantly. Season to taste with salt and pepper. Wrap each dove in a slice of bacon. Cover doves with sauce in deep pan. Bake in 350°F. oven approximately 1 hour. Pour 3/4 cup white wine over the doves, stirring into sauce. Continue to bake until done. Again pour 3/4 cup white wine over doves and serve.

Sauce can be made ahead and kept in refrigerator in a jar.

DOVES COUNTRY STYLE

6 doves
flour
6 rashers bacon
salt, pepper
1 1/2 cups heavy cream
2 teaspoons chopped parsley

Flour birds lightly. Cook bacon in large skillet. Remove and keep warm. Sauté doves in the bacon fat, browning well on all sides. Reduce heat and continue cooking until doves are tender. This will take about 12 minutes. Season to taste. Remove doves to hot platter and garnish with the bacon. Spoon out all but 3 tablespoons fat. Add 4 tablespoons flour and blend well. Cook 3 minutes. Gradually stir in cream and cook, stirring, until smooth and thickened. Season well with salt and pepper, add chopped parsley. Serves 6.

DOVES IN FOIL

Place 6 doves, breast up, on 6 pieces of aluminum foil 12 inches square. Place 1/2 strip thick bacon over breast of each dove. Quarter 4 medium peeled potatoes. Quarter 1 small onion. Cut 1 carrot into 1-inch pieces. Fine-dice 2 1/4-inch slices green pepper. Place vegetables around doves on foil; salt and pepper to taste. Sprinkle 2 tablespoons worcestershire sauce over doves. Fold foil to seal. Bake in 325°F. oven 90 minutes. When done, place foil containers on dinner plate and unfold.

SHERRY-ROASTED DOVES

14 to 16 doves
salt, pepper
flour
1/2 cup salad oil
1/2 cup chopped green onions
1 1/2 cups water
1 cup sherry
1/4 cup chopped parsley

Season doves with salt and pepper. Roll in flour. Place in oil in a heavy roaster. Bake in 400°F. oven until brown. Add onions, water and sherry; cover. Bake until tender, baste with sherry occasionally. Add parsley to gravy just before serving. Serves 8 to 12.

PIGEONS ITALIENNE

4 pigeons
garlic salt, pepper, flour
1/4 cup olive OR salad oil
1 8-ounce can tomato sauce
1/2 cup beer
4 medium onions, sliced
1/4 teaspoon crushed oregano
3 tablespoons chopped parsley

Sprinkle pigeons inside and out with salt, pepper and flour. Heat olive or salad oil in skillet; add pigeons and brown on all sides. Add tomato sauce, beer, onions and oregano. Bring to boil. Cover and cook over low heat 30 to 45 minutes, or until tender. Before serving, stir in parsley. Serves 4.

OVEN-BRAISED DOVES

Brown birds in seasoned flour. Place in dutch oven or casserole. Sprinkle with fine-chopped celery, onion and parsley. Add 1 can mushrooms, plus liquid. Dissolve 2 or 3 chicken bouillon cubes in 2 cups water, and pour over doves. Cover and cook in 325°F. oven 1 1/4 to 1 1/2 hours. Pour 1/2 cup white wine over doves the last 15 minutes of cooking.

PIGEON POT PIE

Simmer 2 dressed pigeons until tender in salted water. Remove bones and cut meat into pieces. In a separate kettle place 2 carrots, 1 large onion, 1 potato, all diced, and cook until tender in a minimum of water. When pigeons and vegetables are cooked, combine and place in a 3-inch deep baking dish, using most of the liquid. Top with Oven Biscuit Topping (below) and bake in 375°F. oven until biscuits are done, about 20 minutes. Serves 3.

Oven Biscuit Topping

2 cups flour
2 1/2 teaspoons baking powder
1/4 teaspoon salt
2 tablespoons shortening
1 scant cup milk

Combine dry ingredients. Cut in shortening. Add milk. Roll dough, cut biscuits and place on top of pigeons and vegetables. Vegetables and meat mixture should be hot before placing biscuits on top. Serves 3 to 4.

COLD PIGEON PIE

6 pigeons, halved
4 tablespoons butter
flour
1 teaspoon salt
1/2 teaspoon white pepper
juice of one lemon
2 cups sherry
1 can mushrooms, drained
4 hard-cooked eggs, sliced
parsley

Draw, clean, and dry pigeons. Melt butter, add pigeons and cook until they are light brown, then pack them in a 4-quart glass baking dish, or any stewing pot that can be tightly covered. Cover with cold water and slowly bring to boiling point. Simmer gently 5 to 6 hours or until done. Remove from the pot. Thicken the gravy with a little flour until the consistency of thin stew—when cold, it will jelly into a thicker consistency. Add salt, pepper and lemon juice to taste; when cool, add sherry. Place birds in a baking dish, scattering in mushrooms and egg slices; add chopped parsley. Cover with gravy, then with pastry (below). Bake in a 350°F. oven 1 hour. Cool, refrigerate overnight. Serves 4 to 6.

Pastry

2 teaspoons baking powder
3 cups flour
1 teaspoon salt
1/2 cup lard
1 1/2 cups milk

Sift the baking powder, flour and salt together. Rub in lard with the tips of the fingers; mix in milk with a knife or spoon. Roll out and cover dish; brush over with milk. Serves 4 to 6.

This pie, with a plain salad, makes a substantial lunch or dinner in winter.

STUFFED WILD PIGEON

6 young pigeons
salt
2 soaked rolls
2 eggs, lightly beaten
1 tablespoon melted butter
1 teaspoon chopped parsley
1/2 cup mushrooms (optional)
4 truffles, minced (optional)
1/4 cup butter
1 cup water
1/2 cup cream
1 teaspoon salt
1 tablespoon flour

Clean pigeons well, wash and dry. Sprinkle with salt inside and out. To make stuffing: Chop the heart, liver and cleaned gizzard very fine. Mix with rolls, eggs,

1 tablespoon butter, parsley, mushrooms and truffles if used; stuff birds; skewer openings or secure with picks, or sew up the opening. Melt the butter in pan and brown birds on all sides, then sauté 1 1/2 hours, adding combined water and cream, a spoonful at a time. When birds are done, place on serving platter. Add salt to gravy and thicken with flour. Serves 6.

POTTED PIGEONS

6 pigeons
any simple bread stuffing
3 slices bacon
1 diced carrot
1 diced onion
chopped parsley
hot water OR stock
1/4 cup fat
1/4 cup flour
buttered toast

Clean and dress the pigeons, stuff and truss, and place them upright in a stewpan on the bacon slices. Add the carrot, onion, and a little parsley; cover with boiling water or stock. Cover the pot tightly and let it simmer 2 to 3 hours or until pigeons are tender, adding boiling water or stock as necessary. Make a sauce of the fat and flour and 2 cups of the stock remaining in the pan. Serve each pigeon on a thin piece of toast and pour gravy over all. Serves 6.

HUNTER'S PIGEON

3 pigeons
1 quart white wine
2 whole peppercorns
1 teaspoon salt
2 cloves
1/2 teaspoon sage
lemon peel
2 tablespoons olive oil

Place pigeons in a casserole with the white wine, peppercorns, salt, cloves, sage, lemon peel, and the olive oil. Cover casserole with aluminum foil and cook in 325°F. oven 3 hours. Serves 3.

BRAISED DOVES

Clean doves, wash and dry; salt and pepper and dredge in flour. Fry in hot frying pan in deep fat. When brown, remove to baking pan. Sprinkle birds with flour again, cover with water, and bake in oven at 350°F. 35 minutes.

PHEASANT

Pheasant can be either dry-plucked or skinned, since it is generally agreed that skinning, which is quicker, does not seriously impair the flavor of these or other upland game birds. However, if the bird is to be roasted, it should be plucked, as the meat of the bird, un-

35

less protected by skin, will seriously dry in roasting. If the pheasant are to be plucked, the feathers should be removed as soon as possible, because they tend to stiffen into the skin when the bird has cooled. This makes them more difficult to pluck.

To skin a pheasant, remove the wings close to the body and the legs at the first joint above the foot. Slit the skin of the bird just under the tail; skin back over the legs and up the body toward the neck. Then break the breast away from the back. The entrails will then stay with the back—which has very little meat on it—and the breast of the bird comes away ready to be wiped and cooked. The legs should be cut away close to the back, and together with the heart, liver and gizzard, should be removed before the bony structure and entrails are discarded. Wipe thoroughly. Pheasant are all white meat and are suitable to use in most recipes for chicken.

CREAM-ROAST PHEASANT

1 young pheasant
salt
butter
2 thin slices bacon
1 cup sweet cream OR sour cream
1 cup water
2 tablespoons flour

Draw the pheasant carefully; wash and dry. Rub inside and out with salt. Put the liver and a piece of butter in the pheasant. Fasten bacon across breast. Bake in 350°F. oven, basting frequently with 4 teaspoons butter. After it has cooked about 30 minutes, baste with cream and water, a spoonful at a time. Pheasant should cook about 1 1/2 hours. Remove bacon before serving. Stir flour into drippings, brown, and add water as needed. Cook 5 minutes. Serve gravy with bird. Serves 4.

PHEASANT PIE

1 pheasant, 3 to 4 pounds
1 bay leaf
1 stalk celery
6 peppercorns
1 tablespoon salt
1/2 cup butter
1/2 cup flour
1 cup light cream
1/8 teaspoon pepper
1/4 teaspoon salt
1 1-pound can pearl onions
1 4-ounce can sliced mushrooms
1 package frozen peas
2 canned pimientos, sliced
1 box pastry mix

Place pheasant in a large kettle and cover with water. Add bay leaf, celery, peppercorns and 1 tablespoon salt. Bring to boil. Cover and cook over low heat 2 to 3 hours, or until pheasant is tender. Remove meat from bones; strain broth. Melt butter in saucepan; add flour and stir until blended. Gradually add 2 cups of the broth, stirring constantly. Add light cream, pepper and salt. Cook, stirring, until thickened. Arrange pheasant pieces, onions, mushrooms, peas and pimientos in a 2-quart casserole. Add sauce to within 1 inch of top. Prepare pastry mix. Cut pastry circle 1/2 inch larger than casserole and place over pheasant mixture, turning edge of pastry under and pressing to casserole with fork or spoon. Garnish top with leaf-shaped pastry cutouts and acorns made by attaching a pastry circle to a filbert with a clove. Bake in preheated 450°F. oven 15 minutes, or until crust is golden brown. Serves 4 to 6.

PHEASANT BAKED IN WINE

Cut cleaned pheasant into 8 or 9 serving pieces, leaving them slightly damp. Season with salt and pepper. Roll pieces in flour and brown in 6 tablespoons hot olive oil until just golden. Sprinkle very lightly on both sides with onion and garlic salt. Remove pieces to a 13- x 9-inch pan. This much can be done a day ahead if desired. Combine 6 tablespoons tomato paste, 6 tablespoons tomato sauce, and 3/4 cup white port. Pour over

pheasant and bake in 250°F. oven 2 hours. If the pheasant is large, weighing close to 4 pounds, bake 2 1/2 hours. Serves 2 to 3.

GOURMET DELIGHT PHEASANT

Use 4 pheasant cut in quarters, OR 4 large breasts. Brown well in butter. Place in baking dish. Pour over 1 cup brandy. Light and let burn out. Add 2 cups chicken stock, 1 onion, chopped, 1 clove garlic, crushed. Season with salt and pepper. Bake in 350°F. oven 1/2 hour, basting several times. Remove from oven and pour over: 1 quart heavy cream or beaten cottage cheese, 1 10-ounce bottle horseradish. Bake 1 1/2 hours. Just before serving, add 1/2 pound mushrooms, sautéed in butter. Serve over wild rice. Serves 6 to 8. *This recipe works equally well using partridge.*

BARBECUED PHEASANT

2 pheasant
flour, salt, pepper
1 large onion, chopped
1 tablespoon butter, melted
1 tablespoon brown sugar
1 tablespoon cornstarch
1/4 cup tomato catsup
2 tablespoons vinegar
2 tablespoons worcestershire sauce
1/4 teaspoon dry mustard
2 cups cooked tomatoes

Cut pheasant into serving pieces and coat with flour to which salt and pepper have been added. Brown in hot fat. Sauté onion in melted butter until tender. Combine brown sugar and cornstarch; blend into onions. Gradually add remaining ingredients and 1/4 teaspoon each salt and pepper, stirring constantly. Cook slowly 20 to 25 minutes or until slightly thickened. Stir frequently. Pour sauce over pheasant; cover. Bake in 300°F. oven 1 1/2 hours, basting with sauce occasionally. Serves 4.

BRAISED PHEASANT WITH CABBAGE

1 pheasant
1/4 pound salt pork in one piece
2 slices fat salt pork
1 teaspoon salt
1/8 teaspoon pepper
1 onion, studded with 4 cloves
1 faggot (2 stalks celery, 4 sprigs parsley, 1/2 bay leaf, sprig of thyme, tied together)
2 cups hot water
1 medium head cabbage (Savoy preferred)
1 carrot
1 knockwurst or frankfurter
1 cup hot water

Cut bird into quarters. Simmer salt pork piece in water to cover for a few minutes. In dutch oven, brown salt pork slices, set aside. Brown quartered bird. Add salt, pepper, onion, faggot, simmered salt pork piece, browned salt pork slices, 2 cups hot water. Simmer, covered, 40 minutes. Meanwhile, separate cabbage leaves; put into kettle with water to cover; simmer 5 minutes. Drain, dip into cold water; drain. To pheasant add cabbage, carrot, knockwurst, 1 cup hot water. Cook, covered, 45 to 60 minutes or until meat is tender and leg separates from body. Serves 4.

FRUIT-ROASTED PHEASANT

1 pheasant
salt, pepper
1 cup wild rice
1 cup apricot juice

Place pheasant on aluminum foil in roaster. Rub interior with salt and pepper; cover with uncooked rice. Pour fruit juice over all. Wrap tightly in the foil. Bake in 325°F. oven until pheasant can be easily pierced with fork. Serves 2 to 4.

PHEASANT A LA MODE

Clean a plump pheasant, removing the breastbone as you would in a small broiler. Rub with a cut lemon inside and out. Sauté the pheasant liver and chop fine. Cube french bread to make 1 1/2 cups; soak in port wine 5 minutes and press dry. Combine with liver; season with onion powder, salt and pepper. Stuff the bird and sew or skewer it up. Marinate in port wine to cover for at least 24 hours. Drain, reserve marinade. Cook in a casserole, with 1/4 pound butter melted in the bottom, in a 350°F. oven until tender, turning the bird often to keep it buttered. Cook 1 1/2 cups of the marinade over high heat until reduced by half. Serve this with the bird, with crusty french bread. Serves 4.

PHEASANT-RICE BAKE

1 pheasant, cut up
1 package dry onion soup mix
1 cup uncooked rice
1 can cream of chicken soup
1 soup-can milk
1 can french fried onion rings

Sprinkle soup mix into buttered 2-quart casserole. Sprinkle rice over soup mix. Add pheasant pieces. Dilute soup with milk and pour over pheasant. Cover, bake in 350°F. oven 1 hour 15 minutes. Uncover, sprinkle with onion rings. Cook 15 minutes longer. Serves 6.

PRESSURE-COOKED PHEASANT

Place clean, disjointed bird in pressure cooker, adding 1 can mushroom soup thinned with 1/2 cup dry sherry in 1/4 cup cream. Cook for 30 minutes after pressure cooker reaches 15 pounds of pressure. Large birds require about 45 minutes.

VIRGINIA PHEASANT WITH SAUCE

2 pheasant, cut into pieces
1/2 cup flour
1 teaspoon salt
1/8 teaspoon pepper
1 teaspoon paprika
1/4 cup butter
1 clove garlic, crushed
1/4 cup chopped ripe olives
1/2 cup water
1/2 teaspoon worcestershire sauce
1/2 cup white wine

Coat pheasant with flour seasoned with salt, pepper, paprika. Brown on all sides in butter in skillet. Add garlic, olives, water and worcestershire sauce; cover tightly. Simmer 45 minutes. Turn pheasant; add wine. Cover; simmer 45 minutes longer or until tender. Serve hot with sauce. Serves 6.

PHEASANT MUSCATEL

3 1 1/2-pound pheasant
1/2 lemon
salt, pepper
1/3 cup butter
juice of 3 oranges (save rinds)
1 cup white raisins
1 teaspoon grated lemon peel
1 cup chicken broth OR stock
1/2 cup muscatel wine

Rinse pheasant inside and out with warm water. Drain; rub insides with lemon and season with salt and pepper. Place in baking dish breast side up; spread with butter. Add orange juice, raisins, lemon peel, chicken stock and wine. Bake in 350°F. oven 45 minutes, basting every 10 minutes. Serve with Nutted Rice in Orange Cups (below). Serves 6.

Nutted Rice in Orange Cups

2 cups chicken broth
1 cup uncooked rice
2 tablespoons butter
2/3 cup chopped pecans
2 tablespoons minced parsley
salt
6 orange shells

In a saucepan, combine chicken broth and rice. Bring to a boil, reduce to simmer and cook for 15 minutes. Remove from heat and stir in butter and remaining ingredients. Fill orange shells.

CURRIED PHEASANT

1 pheasant
1/2 cup flour
3 tablespoons salad oil
2 medium onions, diced
1 1/2 tablespoons curry powder
2 tablespoons flour
3 cups chicken consommé
2 stalks rhubarb, cut in inch-long pieces
2 teaspoons salt

Clean pheasant and cut into 8

pieces. Dredge in flour and cook in hot oil, removing each piece as it browns. Sauté onion in the oil. Mix curry powder and flour and add, stirring until blended and smooth. Add consommé; stir until mixture boils. Replace the meat; add rhubarb and salt. Cover and simmer for 1 1/2 hours, or until tender. Serves 4.

PHEASANT SPANISH STYLE

2 young pheasant,
cut in serving pieces
1/2 cup butter
salt, pepper
2 tablespoons flour
dash of ground cloves
1 1/4 cups game bird stock or chicken bouillon
6 tablespoons frozen orange juice concentrate
2 drops tabasco
1-inch stick cinnamon
3/4 cup white raisins
2/3 cup shredded toasted almonds

Brown birds in melted butter, in large skillet. Season with salt, pepper. Set aside, covered. Blend flour, cloves in butter in skillet. Stir until bubbly. Add stock, orange juice, tabasco sauce; stir and blend until thickened and boiling. Add cinnamon and raisins. Add pheasant to sauce; cover and simmer until tender, 45 minutes or more. Remove stick of cinnamon. Stir in almonds. Serve pheasant on platter mounded with rice that has been cooked in bouillon and flavored with saffron. Pour sauce over birds and serve rest in sauce-boat. Serves 4 to 6.

BRAISED PHEASANT

1 pheasant, cut in serving pieces
1/4 cup cooking oil
1/4 cup lemon juice
1/4 cup vinegar
1 teaspoon garlic salt
1/2 teaspoon tabasco sauce
1/2 teaspoon onion flakes
2 tablespoons parsley flakes

Brown pheasant in hot oil in heavy skillet. Remove from pan. Add seasonings to pan drippings and cook 3 minutes. Add pheasant and cover. Cook over medium heat 1 hour, basting frequently with sauce. Serves 3 to 4.

PHEASANT PAPRIKAS

2 pheasant, cut in serving pieces
bacon drippings
4 cups water
1 teaspoon salt
1/3 teaspoon black pepper
7 bay leaves
2 cloves garlic, minced
3 tablespoons paprika
1 pint sour cream
1/2 teaspoon cornstarch

Brown pheasant pieces well in bacon drippings in deep pan. Add water, salt, pepper, bay leaves, garlic, and sprinkle in paprika. Cook 1 1/2 hours or until pheasant is tender; remove pheasant pieces from stock, and set out 2 cups of gravy to cool. Mix sour cream slowly with the cooled gravy (this prevents curdling) until smooth, then stir into the gravy in pan, with cornstarch, slowly, to prevent lumping. Return pheasant pieces to pan and heat. Serve with egg drop dumpling, mashed potatoes, or browned rice. Serves 4 to 6.

ROAST PHEASANT WITH RICE CAKES

Clean and draw pheasant. Rub insides lightly with salt. Stuff with favorite dressing, and sew up opening with string. Place birds on a rack, breast side up, in a shallow baking pan. Roast in 325°F. oven about 3 hours, or until tender.

Rice Cakes

3 cups cooked, drained rice
2 tablespoons chili sauce
1/2 cup grated sharp cheese
2 eggs
1/2 cup finely rolled cracker crumbs
1 teaspoon salt
dash of pepper
1/4 cup butter
tart jelly

Combine rice, chili sauce, cheese, eggs, half the cracker crumbs, salt, pepper. Mix well. Make into firm cakes, using remaining cracker crumbs. Brown lightly in butter in hot skillet. Top each with spoonful of jelly. Makes 12 2-inch cakes.

PHEASANT AND MUSHROOMS

2 pheasant, cut in serving pieces
1/2 cup pancake mix
1/2 cup butter
2 cups mushrooms, sliced
1 small onion, chopped
2 chicken bouillon cubes, dissolved
in 1 cup hot water
juice of 1/2 lemon
1 teaspoon each: salt, pepper

Roll pieces of pheasant in pancake mix. Sauté in butter until brown. Remove pheasant from skillet; sauté mushrooms and onions in butter until brown. Replace pheasant in skillet. Add bouillon, lemon juice and seasonings. Cover and cook over low heat about 1 hour, or until tender. Serves 6 to 8.

PHEASANT FANTASY

2 pheasant, about 2 1/2 pounds each
salt
Rice Stuffing
4 slices bacon
1/2 cup butter OR margarine, melted

Wipe pheasant inside and out with a damp cloth. Rub cavities with salt, then fill loosely with Rice Stuffing (below). Tie wings and legs to bodies and close openings with skewers. Place breast side up on rack in roasting pan. Lay 2 slices of bacon over each breast. Roast in 350°F. oven 2 hours or until tender, basting frequently with melted butter and pan drippings. Serves 4 to 6.

Rice Stuffing

1 1/3 cups packaged precooked rice
1/4 cup butter
1/4 pound mushrooms, chopped
1 1/4 cups fine-chopped celery and
leaves
1/4 cup fine-chopped onion
1 1/2 teaspoons salt
1/4 teaspoon marjoram
dash of pepper
pinch of sage
pinch of thyme
1 1/3 cups water
1/3 cup chopped pecans

Sauté rice in butter over medium heat until golden brown. Add remaining ingredients, except pecans. Bring quickly to a boil over high heat; then simmer 2 minutes, fluffing rice gently with a fork once or twice. Remove from heat and add pecans. Fluff lightly. Spoon stuffing into pheasant. Roast at once.

LEMON PHEASANT

2 pheasant
6 tablespoons flour
2 teaspoons salt
1/4 teaspoon pepper
6 tablespoons fat
1/4 cup lemon juice
1 10 1/2 ounce can consommé
1 clove garlic, minced
1 1/4 cups water

Cut pheasant into individual servings. Roll in flour, season with salt and pepper. Brown meat well in hot fat in heavy skillet or dutch oven. Add lemon juice, consommé, garlic and water. Cover. Simmer about 1 hour or until tender. Thicken liquid for gravy. Serves 4.

CURRIED PHEASANT CASSEROLE

1 pheasant
2 slices onion
6 whole allspice
1 celery stalk top
1 can condensed cream of celery soup
1/4 cup pheasant broth
1 4-ounce can mushrooms, drained
1/2 teaspoon dried parsley
1/4 teaspoon curry powder
2 tablespoons chopped pimiento
paprika

Cut pheasant in serving pieces; cover with water salted to taste; add onion slices, allspice and celery stalk top. Simmer until tender.

When cool, slice or cube. Combine soup, pheasant broth, mushrooms, parsley, curry powder and pimiento. Add pheasant and mix lightly. Place in buttered casserole, sprinkle with paprika and bake covered in 350°F. oven 40 to 45 minutes. Serve on hot riced potatoes or buttered toast. Serves 4.

PHEASANT A LA MARTIN

2 2- to 3-pound pheasant
4 cups water
1/2 cup vinegar
4 cups chopped celery
2 medium onions, quartered
4 to 6 whole cloves
2-inch piece stick cinnamon
6 teaspoons sugar
1 teaspoon salt
2 bay leaves
salt, pepper
1/2 cup butter

Cut each pheasant in half. Combine water and next 8 ingredients in large bowl. Marinate pheasant halves in mixture for 12 hours, turning occasionally. Remove pheasant; dry well. Reserve marinade. Sprinkle pheasant with salt and pepper. Brown in hot butter in large skillet. Add the 2 cups of reserved marinade. Simmer, covered, about 1 hour, or until pheasant is tender. Add more marinade during cooking, if necessary. Serves 4 to 6.

PHEASANT MULLIGAN WITH DUMPLINGS

2 young pheasant
2 cups diced carrots
1 cup diced onions
1 cup fine-shredded cabbage
2 cups diced potatoes
2 tablespoons fat
salt, pepper

Clean pheasant, cut into serving portions and cover with water. Add carrots, onions and cabbage and cook slowly until nearly tender. Add potatoes, fat, salt and pepper. Cook until meat and vegetables are tender. Add dumplings (below). Cook for 15 minutes without lifting the cover. Serves 8.

Dumplings

2 cups sifted flour
3 teaspoons baking powder
1/2 teaspoon salt
1 egg
3/4 cup milk

Sift flour, baking powder and salt together; beat egg, add milk and stir into dry ingredients, adding more milk, if necessary, to form a drop batter. Drop by tablespoons into the hot mulligan and cover kettle tightly.

BATTER FRIED HUNTER-STYLE PHEASANT

Pluck, singe, draw and wash pheasant thoroughly. Cut in pieces for serving or cut in half. Cover with water to which 1 teaspoon salt has been added and cook until almost tender. Cool and dip in batter made by whipping together until smooth: 1 1/2 cups flour, 1/2 teaspoon salt, 1 1/2 cups beer. Fry over moderate heat 30 minutes.

SMOKEY PHEASANT

1 pheasant
1/2 cup lightly fried pork sausage
1/2 cup chopped apple
1/8 teaspoon salt
1/2 teaspoon chopped onion
dash pepper
1 cup breadcrumbs
1/3 cup hot water

Wash pheasant; wipe dry. Sprinkle inside with salt. Mix together all other ingredients; stuff loosely into cavity. Close opening with skewers and lace shut. Sprinkle entire pheasant with salt and place breast side down on rack in roaster. Cover pan with aluminum foil. Roast at 325°F. 30 minutes. Mix 1/2 cup melted butter with 1/4 teaspoon liquid smoke seasoning and baste pheasant. Turn breast side up for remainder of roasting; baste with smoke-butter mixture every 15 minutes until tender. Keep covered until last few minutes when cover may be removed to brown pheasant. Serves 4.

The aluminum foil cover allows the smoke aroma to penetrate the meat, giving it a delicious flavor.

ORANGE-KISSED PHEASANT

1 pheasant cut in serving pieces
1/3 cup flour
3/4 teaspoon seasoned salt
1/4 teaspoon pepper
3/4 teaspoon paprika
1 teaspoon sugar
1/2 teaspoon ginger
1/4 cup vegetable shortening
1/4 cup butter
2 tablespoons grated orange rind
1 cup fresh-squeezed orange juice
1 teaspoon lemon juice
1/2 cup crushed pineapple

Wash pheasant, drain and pat dry. Combine flour and seasonings, and place in a plastic bag. Shake pheasant, a few pieces at a time, in the bag. Melt shortening and butter in a heavy skillet and brown pheasant on all sides. Arrange pheasant in a single layer in a casserole or baking dish. Cover pheasant with grated orange rind, mixed orange and lemon juices, and pineapple. Cover pan. Bake in 375°F. oven until tender, about 1 hour. Place pheasant pieces in deep serving dish, pour pan juices over all, and garnish with orange wedges, pepper rings. Serves 4.

PHEASANT DELMONICO

Wash and cut pheasant in serving pieces. Dry and brush with melted butter. Season with salt and pepper. Place 1 cup biscuit mix in paper bag. Add pheasant pieces and shake. Remove pheasant and place in roaster. Pour over 1/2 cup melted butter. Cover roaster and bake in 350°F. oven 1 to 1 1/2 hours. Remove from oven; place thin slices of processed cheese over the bird. Reduce oven temperature to 250° and return uncovered roaster to oven for 15 to 20 minutes or until cheese is melted and slightly brown.

OVEN-FRIED PARMESAN PHEASANT

1 cup herb-seasoned stuffing, crushed
2/3 cup grated parmesan cheese
1/4 cup fine-chopped parsley
1 2 1/2-pound pheasant, cut in serving pieces
1/2 cup melted butter

Combine crushed stuffing, cheese and parsley. Dip pheasant pieces in melted butter; then roll in stuffing mixture. Arrange pieces, skin side up, in large shallow pan. Do not crowd or turn. Sprinkle with remaining crumbs and butter. Bake in 375°F. oven 1 hour or until tender. Serves 4.

BAKED PHEASANT

Clean and cut up pheasant for frying. Wipe thoroughly, dip in flour, and brown in butter in a frying pan. Place in roaster, sprinkle with salt and pepper. Put enough sour cream in pan to make 1 inch in depth and add 1/8 pound of butter for each bird. Cover and bake in 300°F. oven from 1 1/2 to 2 hours, or until birds are tender. Make a gravy and cover birds before serving.

PHEASANT EPICURE WITH WILD RICE

4 breasts of pheasant, split
8 legs of pheasant, thighs and
drumsticks
1/2 cup flour
1 teaspoon salt
1/4 teaspoon pepper
3/4 cup milk
1/4 pound butter
2 cups stock
1 medium onion, fine-chopped
3/4 cup sherry OR muscatel wine
1 pint sour cream

Clean birds thoroughly, cut in serving pieces, split breasts, and dry. Mix flour, salt and pepper. Dip pieces of meat in milk, then in flour mixture. Lay on paper towel. Melt 3/4 stick of butter in a heavy skillet. Sauté floured meat until nicely browned. Drain off excess fat and add stock. Simmer meat 1 hour. Meanwhile, melt remainder of butter; cook onions in this until light brown. Add flour remaining from meat, add wine and onions. Cover tightly and cook slowly until tender. Taste for seasoning. Just before serving break down sour cream with a fork and add to meat. Reheat until it bubbles up. Place on a large deep platter, pour sauce over meat. Serve with Wild Rice Mold (below). Serves 6 to 8.

Wild Rice Mold

Wash 2 cups wild rice; soak overnight in warm water. Drain off water and measure into saucepan enough water to make 1 quart. Add wild rice, 1/2 cup long grain rice and 1 teaspoon salt. Bring the rice to a boil and simmer, covered, until both kinds of rice are done. Butter a large ring mold and pack rice in tightly, being sure all liquid has been absorbed. Set over hot water to keep hot. When serving, turn out on chop plate. Fill center of mold with sautéed fresh mushrooms.

ROAST PHEASANT WITH PURPLE PLUM SAUCE

2 young pheasant
1 onion, halved
2 stalks celery
2 apple slices
4 bacon slices
salt, pepper

Place onion, celery and apple slices inside birds, 2 strips bacon over each breast. Season with salt and pepper. Roast in 350°F. oven 2 hours, basting with Plum Sauce (below) during last half hour of roasting. Serve remaining sauce in sauceboat. Serves 4 to 6.

Plum Sauce

1 1-pound can purple plums
1/4 cup butter
1/4 cup chopped onion
3 tablespoons lemon juice
1/4 cup brown sugar
2 tablespoons chili sauce
1 teaspoon worcestershire sauce
1/2 teaspoon ginger

Drain plums and reserve liquid. Remove pits from plums and purée in blender. Melt butter in small saucepan; add onion and sauté until golden. Stir in remaining ingredients, including plums and liquid. Simmer 30 minutes.

ROAST PHEASANT WITH CREAM SAUCE

Start heating oven to 450°F. Heat a shallow open pan in oven. Tie legs and wings of pheasant close to body with string. Sprinkle with salt and pepper. Completely cover breast with slices of salt pork or bacon; tie with string. Place bird on side in heated pan; pour 1/4 cup salad oil over all. Roast bird un-covered 15 minutes, basting often. Turn on other side, repeat. (Bird is done when juice, which runs out when bird is lifted from pan and held tail down, is clear, without pink tinge.) Remove bird from pan; cut away string. Pour off fat from pan; add about 3/4 cup of water to pan and simmer, stirring to loosen brown bits. Simmer until liquid is reduced to about 1/2 cup. Season with salt and pepper, quickly stir in 1 tablespoon butter; remove gravy from heat as soon as butter is melted. Slice meat from pheasant; serve on toast with Quick Cream Sauce (below), and the gravy.

Quick Cream Sauce for Game

2 tablespoons butter
2 teaspoons minced onion OR
shallots
2 teaspoons flour
1 teaspoon lemon juice
1 1/2 cups heavy cream
2 teaspoons currant OR other
red jelly
salt

Melt butter, stir in onion and flour, cook 1 to 2 minutes. Add lemon juice; slowly add the cream and cook, stirring only until blended and thickened. Add jelly. Taste and add salt if needed. Put over slices of meat on toast or serve separately in sauceboat.
Use this recipe for grouse also.

WATERFOWL

Waterfowl, when brought to the table, offer the hunter pleasure at least as great as his earlier pleasure in bagging them. Duck hunting has always been so popular that at one time ducks were threatened with extinction. Conservation measures now protect them to make sure that water birds can be enjoyed by all.

Follow the rules for all game birds. Draw as soon as possible after the birds are shot. Body heat should be allowed to dissipate as rapidly as possible. The waterfowl should be kept cool until they are cooked.

There is a good deal of controversy concerning the roasting of wild ducks. Some connoisseurs maintain that they should be served very rare—cooked only briefly in a hot oven—barely warmed up, detractors of this type of cooking complain. There are others who believe that a duck is not edible unless it is well done; however, this type of roasting produces a drier, less palatable bird. A happy medium suits most people—for a duck of medium size, about three-quarters of an hour in a moderate oven produces a flavorful, juicy bird.

An older bird should be cooked by a moist method—any braising recipe works well for such a duck. Young ducks can be determined in the early part of the season by the slight continuation of the stem of the tail feathers, which will extend about an eighth of an inch beyond the fibers. This is a certain indication that the bird is young and will take well to roasting. As for numbers of servings, count on a duck serving two—like its domestic brother, most of a wild duck's meat is on its breast and thighs; wings and drumsticks and backs yield very little that is edible.

When hanging, awaiting transportation, birds may be placed in individual paper bags to protect them from insects and from dust. At the end of the hunting trip, they should be packed in dry ice to be shipped to their final destination in a sealed container. For more details about packing and shipping these as well as all other game birds, see page 168.

COOT, MUD HEN

Coot live on many of the same foods as other waterfowl and make an excellent dish when properly handled and prepared. All too often people turn up their noses at coot when in reality they are missing a most tasty wild fowl dish. They are easier to prepare than duck, since they should always be skinned—the skin has a strong taste. After skinning, *all* fat must be removed. Then soak coot in salt solution to which 2 tablespoons of vinegar have been added, for 4 to 6 hours before cooking.

BRAISED COOT
6 coot
1 dozen onions
bacon fat
salt

Skin coot. Clean, and cut off head, feet, wings, and tail. Rinse in cold water. Slice onions. Use a frying pan large enough to handle coot, onions and stirring action without spilling over. Place frying pan on low heat and add a generous amount of bacon fat. When fat is melted, add onions to cover the bottom of the pan, then add pieces of coot. Add salt to taste, and place cover on pan. Cook on low heat until done, stirring occasionally. If necessary, add a little water to prevent scorching. Serves 5.

COOT NEW HAVEN

3 coot
1 fresh lime
1 teaspoon salt
3 stalks celery
2 cups green beans, cooked
1 can condensed cream of mushroom
soup (undiluted)
2 cups whipped cream
parmesan cheese

Rub the breasts and legs of birds with freshly cut lime and set in refrigerator overnight. Rinse, place in kettle with water to cover, add salt and celery. Simmer until meat falls from bones. Cut meat into small pieces and discard bones along with stock. Place beans in casserole, top with coot meat. Over this pour the mushroom soup. Heat thoroughly in oven—no further cooking is required. Top with layer of whipped cream and sprinkle with parmesan cheese. Serve immediately. Serves 2.

MUD HENS
WITH CREAM GRAVY

Tie necks of hens, then make a slit over the beast, piercing only skin. Pull skin, plumage and all, from body. Draw, wash thoroughly and let soak about 3 hours in water to which has been added a handful of salt and 1/2 cup vinegar. In each hen, place a piece of onion and a piece of apple. Tie with cord, so fowl retains its shape. Cover with cold water and simmer about 10 minutes. Drain, add salt, pepper and paprika to taste and tie a strip of bacon on breast of each fowl. Heat 1 tablespoon butter in deep kettle, place hens in this, breast down. Cover tightly and cook slowly from 1 1/2 to 2 hours until tender. Add 1 1/2 cups water to giblets and simmer until reduced to 3/4 cup stock; gradually add this to hens the last 15 minutes. Add 2 tablespoons thick sour cream to gravy. Heat through, but do not boil.

COOT STEW

2 coot
6 medium onions
5 carrots, cut in 1-inch pieces
5 tomatoes, peeled, diced
pinch of marjoram
2 tablespoons chopped parsley
1 tablespoon salt
1 teaspoon pepper
2 bay leaves
1 quart water
3 tablespoons vinegar

Skin birds, removing all fat. Cut out breast, legs and thighs; discard remainder. Place all other ingredients in large, heavy kettle. Bring to simmer. Salt and pepper the coot, roll in flour, brown in butter in skillet. Pour into kettle with vegetables, simmer slowly, covered, about 2 hours. Serves 2.

BRAISED MUD HENS

Cut 3 to 4 hens in serving pieces. Season with salt and pepper. Coat with flour; brown in half oil, half butter. When meat is browned, pour off fat. Cover hens with water; add 1/2 cup sherry, 3 onions cut in small pieces, 1/4 cup celery cut fine. Cover pan and simmer until tender. Serves 5 to 6.

DUCK

It is generally considered better to pluck ducks than to skin them, as skinned birds are likely to prove drier and less flavorful. Remove wings at joint nearest body, and legs at first joint above feet. Pull out all larger feathers near wings and tail and pick duck roughly. Paraffin and water will do a neat job of removing feathers. For six ducks, place 3 12-ounce cakes paraffin in a pot with 6 quarts of water. Heat to about 160°F.—if too hot, little paraffin will cling to the bird. Immerse ducks one by one so that a coating of paraffin adheres to the feathers. Dip each bird two or three times, allowing paraffin to harden between dippings. When final dipping has hardened, small feathers and down may be easily removed by scraping with a small knife. Paraffin may be reused several times by removing feathers each time it is heated. If paraffin is not available, birds should be plucked as clean as possible and singed to remove remaining down.

Ducks should be drawn at the earliest opportunity, particularly in warm weather. To remove entrails, make a cut starting just to the rear of the breastbone and around the vent. This allows easy removal of entrails, including large intestine, gizzard, heart, lungs and liver. The empty cavity should be cleaned thoroughly, preferably by wiping out with a cloth soaked in cold water and wrung almost dry. The heart, liver, and gizzard are well worth saving—to be used, cooked and chopped, in stuffing or gravy—and they, too, should be wiped thoroughly. Do not use livers or gizzards that have been penetrated by shot.

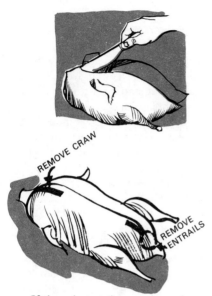

If there is not time to do a thorough job of drawing the ducks soon after they are shot, it is wise to remove the craw and the intestines, at least. This can be done by making a small opening at the neck and another at the anus. A buttonhook or a wire bent into a hook can be pushed into the opening to withdraw intestines. Or a small fork of a limb from any tough shrub or small tree may be used. Cut off one branch of the fork close to the crotch, making a sharp point. Insert this, using the longer branch as a handle and, twisting, pull out the intestines. Removal of craw and intestines will go a long

way toward insuring good keeping quality for your ducks.

After ducks have been plucked and drawn, a thorough washing inside and out in cold water, followed by soaking cleaned birds in very cold water overnight, then wiping dry with a clean cloth or paper toweling, will ready the birds for wrapping or freezing. Double wrap with freezer wrap.

Feathers should be left on ducks that are to be hung immediately or to be shipped without refrigeration in ordinary ice. When shipping ducks in this manner, it is best to stuff the body cavity with dry grass or clean crumpled paper. However, ducks should be plucked before they are frozen as it is more difficult to pluck a bird that has once been frozen and allowed to thaw. When shipped with dry ice, the birds should be cleaned, plucked and frozen before they are shipped. See instructions for shipping, page 168. In the following recipes, all weights for birds are dressed weights.

REMINGTON MALLARDS

Place ducks in pan breast up. Sprinkle each duck with 1 tablespoon of cooking sherry. Season each with:

> *1/2 teaspoon celery salt*
> *1/2 teaspoon onion salt*
> *1/2 teaspoon celery seed*
> *1/4 teaspoon curry powder*
> *1 teaspoon salt*
> *1/4 teaspoon pepper*
> *Let stand in pan 1/2 to 1 hour.*

Chop 1 small onion and 1 stalk celery and place in pan. Add 1/4 to 1/2 inch of water. Bake at 500°F. until breast is brown (about 20 minutes). Turn and bake until back is brown. Cover and cook one hour at 300°F. Total cooking time, about 2 hours. If stuffing is desired, use any favorite poultry stuffing recipe.

During hunting season, Kelsor Smith, Remington's famous chef, receives many requests for this mouth-watering recipe.

LEMON-ROASTED DUCK

> *4 mallards*
> *salt, pepper*
> *1 stick butter*
> *juice and rind of 2 lemons*

Wash the ducks both inside and out, dry completely. Salt and pepper. Melt butter in roasting pan; brown ducks on all sides on top of stove. Pour lemon juice in cavities of ducks and put rind around sides. Cook, covered, in 300°F. oven until tender. Remove meat from bones and pour gravy in pan over meat. Serves 6.

WILD DUCK WITH PECAN STUFFING

> *2 2 1/2-pound wild ducks*
> *4 cups soft breadcrumbs*
> *1 cup fine-chopped celery*
> *1 cup fine-chopped onion*
> *1 cup seedless raisins*
> *1 cup pecan meats, chopped*
> *1/2 teaspoon salt*
> *1/2 cup milk, scalded*
> *2 eggs, beaten*
> *6 slices bacon*
> *1 cup tomato catsup*
> *1/4 cup worcestershire sauce*
> *1/4 cup A-1 Sauce*
> *1/2 cup chili sauce*

Mix breadcrumbs, celery, onions, raisins, nuts and salt together. Add hot milk to beaten eggs and then add to dry mixture. Fill ducks with this stuffing. Close slits by using poultry pins or by sewing. Place in roaster and cover each duck with 3 strips bacon. Roast uncovered in 350°F. oven, allowing 15 to 20 minutes per pound. Twenty minutes before serving, combine last 4 ingredients and baste ducks with this sauce. Garnish with parsley and slices of orange with a few candied cranberries in center of each slice. Skim fat from sauce and serve sauce with ducks. Serves 4.

SMOTHERED DUCK

1 duck
1 teaspoon salt
1/4 teaspoon pepper
1/2 teaspoon thyme
1/2 cup flour
1/2 cup salad oil
1 cup half-and-half
1 small onion, stuck with 2 cloves

Cut cleaned duck into pieces. Mix salt, pepper, thyme and flour. Dredge duck with this mixture. Fry duck slowly in hot oil until brown on both sides, about 30 minutes, turning only once. Add half-and-half and onion; cover tightly and bake for 1 hour, or until tender, in a 325°F. oven. Serves 3 to 4.

ROAST WILD DUCK WITH RAISIN-ORANGE STUFFING

3 wild ducks
1/2 cup light OR dark raisins
2 teaspoons instant minced onion,
OR 3 tablespoons fine-chopped
raw onion
3/4 cup thin-sliced celery
1/4 cup butter
2 teaspoons grated orange rind
1/2 teaspoon salt
1/4 teaspoon powdered thyme
dash of pepper
3 cups soft breadcrumbs

Clean ducks, wash inside and out, and pat dry with paper towels. Rinse and drain raisins. If instant minced onion is used, combine with 1 tablespoon water and let stand a few minutes. Cook onion and celery slowly in butter about 5 minutes. Add orange rind, salt, thyme and pepper. Pour over breadcrumbs, tossing to blend. Fill ducks with stuffing; tie legs and wings. Place stuffed duck on rack in roasting pan. Roast in 450°F. oven about 30 minutes. Remove strings and place ducks on heated platter. Garnish if desired with watercress, orange slices and whole cooked prunes. Serve with Orange Sauce (below). Serves 6.

Orange Sauce

2 tablespoons flour
2/3 cup orange juice
1 teaspoon grated orange rind
1 teaspoon grated lemon rind

Pour most of the fat from roasting pan. Add 1/2 cup hot water to pan, and stir to incorporate rich brown drippings. Thicken with flour; cook, stirring, until thick and smooth. Blend in orange juice and heat. Sprinkle with orange and lemon rind.

WILD DUCK ON TOAST

wild duck
1 tablespoon salt
1 tablespoon baking soda
quarters of apples, oranges, onions,
celery stalks
4 strips bacon
1/2 cup red burgundy
4 slices toasted bread
1 tablespoon anchovy paste
1/4 cup butter
4 slices baked ham
button mushrooms sautéed in butter

Allow 1/2 duck for each person. Soak duck 3 hours in cold water to which has been added 1 tablespoon salt and 1 tablespoon baking soda. Rinse and drain thoroughly. Salt and pepper each duck; fill each cavity with quartered apple, orange, onion and celery. Cover each breast with 2 strips bacon. Place uncovered in 400°F. oven 15 minutes. Cover, and reduce heat to 325°F. After 15 minutes add burgundy; cover and continue cooking. Baste frequently. Cook at least 3 hours. When done remove breastbone and split in half. Spread each slice of toasted bread with anchovy paste mixed with butter. Place a slice of ham on each piece of toast and then a roast duck half. Garnish with mushrooms.

This is a rich and hearty dish. A fresh vegetable and a simple salad complete the meal.

ROAST STUFFED WILD DUCK

Clean duck, rub inside with salt and pepper. Fill loosely with stuffing (below). Place breast side up for roasting. Wrap wings in bacon strips to keep them from drying out. Roast, uncovered, in 350°F. oven, about 25 minutes per pound. Serves 2.

Stuffing

2 cups ground meat (pork and beef)
4 tablespoons butter
salt, pepper
2 cups breadcrumbs (soak and press dry)
1/2 cup milk OR cream
2 tablespoons onion

MALLARD DUCKS IN GRAND MARNIER SAUCE

Trim the wing tips and cut off the necks of 3 or 4 wild ducks. Wash thoroughly, inside and out, with cold water; dry. Rub cavities with lemon juice, and in each put a few celery leaves and 1 onion, sliced. Place ducks breast up on rack in shallow baking pan. Cook birds in 325°F. oven 1/2 hour. Drain fat from pan and add 1 1/2 cups dry white wine. Baste ducks and continue cooking 1 1/2 hours, basting with pan juices every 20 minutes. If a very crisp skin is desired, brush ducks with 1 tablespoon honey about 15 minutes before taking them from the oven and do not baste again. Remove ducks to hot serving platter, and keep warm. Skim excess fat from juices in roasting pan. In heavy saucepan combine 1/2 cup sugar and 1 tablespoon wine vinegar. Cook mixture over medium flame until sugar melts and begins to carmelize. Add juice of 2 oranges, 1/2 cup Grand Marnier, and grated rind of 1 orange. Stir well and cook 5 minutes. Combine this mixture with juices in roasting pan and add 1/4 cup orange peel cut in julienne strips, cooked in a little water for 5 minutes and drained. Season to taste and pour sauce over ducks on serving platter.

BRAISED DUCK WITH RED CABBAGE

1 3-pound wild duck
1 tablespoon baking soda
1/3 cup shortening OR drippings
for frying
1 1/2 teaspoons salt
1/4 teaspoon pepper
1/2 cup flour
1 cup water
1 medium head red cabbage,
coarse-cut
1/2 cup vinegar
2 tablespoons sugar

Remove pinfeathers and singe. Rub 1 tablespoon baking soda into skin of duck, then rinse thoroughly in several changes of warm water. Drain. Cut into serving pieces. Heat shortening in aluminum skillet (do not use iron, as the reaction of the vinegar may darken cabbage). Put salt, pepper and flour in a clean paper bag. Put in a few pieces of duck at a time and shake until each piece is well coated with flour mixture. Brown on all sides in hot shortening over medium heat. Add 1/2 cup water. Cover tightly and simmer gently about 1 hour. Lift up pieces of duck, lay the cabbage on the bottom of the skillet and replace the duck on top. Add vinegar, sugar and remaining 1/2 cup water. Cover and continue to cook until cabbage and duck are tender (45 minutes to 1 hour). Arrange cabbage and duck on a platter, boil liquid left in pan vigorously for a few minutes to obtain a thin gravy-like consistency. Pour over cabbage and serve at once. Serves 2.

BARTON'S DUCK-ON-THE-SPIT

Marinate ducks in olive oil with sliced onions, juniper berries and thyme, turning them several times over a period of hours. Split through the middle from head to tail and run steel knitting needles through the birds to steady them on the spit. Roast about 18 minutes over fairly good charcoal heat. At end of roasting time, flame by bringing up the charcoal bed and pouring cognac over birds. This crisps the skin.

HUNGARIAN ROAST DUCK

2 wild ducks, 2 to 2 1/2 pounds
garlic salt, pepper
2 tablespoons paprika
2 apples, quartered
2 onions, quartered
6 slices bacon
1/4 cup butter, melted
3 cups sauerkraut
4 juniper berries, crushed
2 teaspoons caraway seed
2 slices cooked bacon, crumbled

Sprinkle ducks inside and out with salt, pepper and paprika. Place apple and onion quarters in cavity of each. Cover breasts with bacon and fasten with string. Place ducks breast up in baking pan. Roast in 350°F. oven 1 to 1 1/4 hours, or 15 minutes per pound, basting frequently with butter. Combine sauerkraut, juniper berries, caraway seed and bacon in shallow casserole. Mix well. Place in oven 20 minutes before ducks are done. Discard apple and onion quarters; remove string. Carve ducks. Arrange duck slices on sauerkraut. Serves 4.

Serve with potato pancakes, plum jelly, hot biscuits. This is equally delicious warmed over.

CANTONESE DUCK

2 wild ducks, 2 to 2 1/2 pounds
garlic salt, pepper
4 sprigs parsley
1 lemon, halved
6 slices bacon
1/2 cup beer
1/4 cup dry mustard
1/2 teaspoon monosodium
glutamate
2 tablespoons soy sauce
1 cup apricot preserves
1 tablespoon lemon juice
1 teaspoon grated orange peel
1/4 cup butter, melted

Sprinkle ducks inside and out with salt and pepper. Place 2 sprigs parsley and 1/2 lemon in cavity of each. Cover breasts with bacon and fasten with string. For Cantonese sauce, stir beer into dry mustard. Stir in remaining ingredients except butter and heat in double boiler over hot water. Place ducks breast up in baking pan. Roast in 350°F. oven 15 minutes per pound, basting frequently with butter and once with Cantonese sauce. Carve ducks. Serve with rice, remaining Cantonese sauce. Serves 4.

DUCKS MEXICO IN WINE

Rub 2 dressed ducks inside and out with wood ashes and then wash. Place a lighted charcoal inside duck until it extinguishes. Fry duck to brown, then place in saucepan with

2 quarts of water, salt, pepper, 1 garlic clove, 1 whole onion, 2 cups red wine. Cover pan and let simmer at low heat until ducks are tender. When they are done, add a thick mushroom sauce to juices in pan. Serve with breasts cut in slices and covered with sauce. May be served on toast points. Serves 4.

SAUSAGE-STUFFED WILD DUCK

Rub inside of duck lightly with salt. Put stuffing (below) lightly into cavity and skewer or lace opening. Brush outside with soft shortening and dust with flour. Place in covered roasting pan, breast side up, and roast in 325°F. oven 3 1/2 to 4 hours, or until breast meat starts to fall off bone. Baste at 45-minute intervals, and season with salt, pepper. Serves 2.

Stuffing

1/2 pound unseasoned pork sausage
1/4 cup grated onion
1/2 cup fine-cut celery
1 tablespoon minced parsley
2 tablespoons grated green pepper
1 1/2 cups cold water
1/2 teaspoon pepper
1 teaspoon salt
4 cups dry bread cubes
1/2 teaspoon sage OR poultry seasoning
1/4 cup melted butter

Mix well first 8 ingredients and cook 40 to 45 minutes. Remove from heat and cool until grease sets. Remove as much of the grease as possible. Add bread cubes, sage or poultry seasoning, melted butter. Toss to mix well, adding more moisture if necessary.

WILD DUCK BURGUNDY

Clean and dress duck. Stuff with slices of onion, apple, orange, celery and, if desired, 1/2 clove of garlic. Rub breast with soy sauce and salad oil mixed in equal amounts. Place in baking pan and roast uncovered in 450°F. oven, basting often with burgundy (about 1/2 cup per duck). Roasting time: rare, 15 to 20 minutes; well done, 45 minutes. Remove stuffing before serving.

ROASTED DUCK BREASTS

breasts of 3 wild ducks
flour
salt, pepper
1/2 cup chopped celery
1 onion, chopped
1/4 pound butter
1 1/2 teaspoon poultry seasoning
1 cup water
1 package prepared stuffing mix

Roll duck in flour, seasoned with salt and pepper. Brown in hot oil. Cook celery and onions in butter. Stir in poultry seasoning. Add 1 cup water. Stir in prepared stuffing mix. More water may be added to make the dressing moist. Put in small roaster. Place browned breasts over dressing. Pour any oil left in pan over the ducks. Cover and bake in 350°F. oven 1 hour. Serves 2.

BROILED TEAL

Prepare 3 teal for cooking. Split into halves without completely dividing. Season with 1 teaspoon salt, 1/2 teaspoon pepper. Roll teal well in vegetable oil, and broil under a clean, but not too hot, flame 10 minutes on each side. Serves 3.

BROILED WILD DUCK

Split the ducks and rub them well with soy sauce and a little tarragon or rosemary. For rare duck, broil under a hot flame, watching carefully, for about 6 minutes on the bone side and 4 to 6 minutes on the skin side. Be sure not to burn the skin. Baste with butter and soy sauce or butter and white wine. Season to taste.

ORANGE-ROASTED WILD DUCK

Soak wild duck in buttermilk for 5 hours. Rinse thoroughly. Stuff each duck with 1 orange cut in quarters, 2 celery stalks, and a small onion. Bake in 325°F. oven 3 hours or until done. Baste every 30 minutes with orange juice; during last half hour baste with orange marmalade. Discard stuffing. Make gravy from pan juices.

CHINESE DUCKS

2 large ducks
2 onions, chopped
1 teaspoon dry ginger
cooking oil
1 teaspoon salt
pepper
1 teaspoon Chinese 5 spices
1/4 cup white wine
2 teaspoons sugar
1/2 dried orange peel
1 teaspoon salt
1 teaspoon caraway seed
1/2 teaspoon aniseed

Clean and pat duck cavities dry. Sauté onions and ginger in oil until onions are transparent. Add 1 teaspoon salt, pepper, Chinese 5 spices, white wine, sugar; mix well. Stuff cavities of ducks with this mixture and close with skewers. Seal skin of ducks by pouring boiling water over entire body until skin ceases to draw. Rub ducks with oil and brown. Place ducks in large, deep pan and fill with water to 1/2 inch of top of breasts. Add to the water the orange peel, salt, caraway seed, anise seed. Bring water to a boil, lower heat and simmer for 2 hours. Serves 4.

MALLARD WITH WILD RICE DRESSING

2 mallards
1 cup wild rice
2 teaspoons salt
2 tablespoons minced onion
2 tablespoons minced green pepper
2 tablespoons minced celery
1 4-ounce can chopped
mushrooms, drained
1/4 teaspoon pepper
1/4 pound butter, melted
2 cups orange juice

Cook wild rice in 1 quart water with 1 teaspoon salt 40 minutes. Drain off unabsorbed water, and dry rice by spreading on towel or shaking pan over low fire. To the rice add the onion, pepper, celery, mushrooms, 1 teaspoon salt, the pepper and the melted butter. Stuff the mallards with this dressing and roast in 350°F. oven 2 hours. Baste frequently with the orange juice mixed with equal parts of water. Remove any excessive grease that collects each time, before basting, with a bulb-type baster. Serves 4.

DUCK CASSOULET

1 1/2 cups dry white beans
1/2 pound salt pork, diced
1/3 cup flour
salt, pepper
2 medium ducks, cut in
serving pieces
1 medium onion, chopped
1 clove garlic, crushed
1 1/2 teaspoons salt
1/4 teaspoon pepper
dash of cloves
1/2 teaspoon mustard
2 peppercorns
1/4 cup catsup

Soak beans overnight; drain. Cook in salted water for about 1 1/2 hours, drain and place in casserole. Blanch salt pork briefly in boiling water; drain and fry slowly in a heavy skillet. Remove pork pieces and reserve. Season the flour with salt and pepper and dredge the duck pieces. Brown in hot salt-pork fat. Remove to casserole. Cook onion and garlic in the same pan about 10 minutes. Add 1 1/2 teaspoons salt, 1/4 teaspoon pepper, remaining seasonings, reserved cooked salt pork and 1 1/2 cups water; bring to a boil and pour over beans and meat, adding hot water as needed to cover well. Bake, covered, in 350°F. oven for 1 1/2 to 2 hours, or until meat is tender and beans are cooked. Serve from casserole with green salad and crusty bread. Serves 6.

DUCK SOUP

*1 large OR 2 small ducks, cut
into small pieces
8 cups water
2 stalks celery with leaves, chopped
1 large carrot, shredded
1 large onion, diced
1 teaspoon salt
6 chicken bouillon cubes*

Place all in large kettle. Simmer gently 2 to 3 hours. If too thick, add 1 cup water. Add 2 to 3 ounces thin noodles. Cook very slowly 1/2 hour longer.

Like most soups, this one is improved by reheating.

FOIL-ROASTED WILD DUCK

*1 duck
salt, pepper
1 onion
1/4 cup red wine
1/2 teaspoon thyme
1 pat butter*

Rub inside of duck with salt and pepper. Put onion inside. Place on large piece of heavy foil, and pour wine over. Sprinkle thyme on duck and place a pat of butter on it. Wrap closely. Bake in 325°F. oven 3 1/2 hours. Serve with wild rice. Serves 2.

The juices in the foil after baking are delicious with crusty bread.

BROILED BREAST OF TEAL

Use only the breasts; flatten each piece slightly with rolling pin. Melt 4 tablespoons butter and add to it 1 teaspoon lemon juice and 1/4 teaspoon white pepper. Broil breasts 10 minutes on each side, brushing frequently with butter-lemon mixture. When nearly done, pour over breasts 1 can sliced, broiled mushrooms; run under heat just long enough to finish breasts and heat mushrooms. Pour any remaining lemon-butter over all.

DUCK A LA KING

*1 cup or more leftover duck meat,
cut in small pieces
1 small can mushrooms, drained
1/2 green pepper, diced
1 pimiento, diced (optional)
1 can peas, drained
1/2 cup butter
1/2 cup flour
2 cups chicken bouillon (4 cubes)
1/2 cup cream*

Toss first 6 ingredients in bowl and season with salt and pepper. Melt butter in saucepan. Add flour, stir until smooth. Add chicken bouillon, stir smooth. Add cream, stir in duck mixture. Serve with rice or on toast. Serves 2.

STUFFED ROTISSERIE DUCK

1 or 2 ducks, depending on size
1 tablespoon aniseed
1 tablespoon ground coriander
1 medium onion
3/4 pound ground beef
1 tablespoon butter
1 cup raisins
1 teaspoon coriander
1 teaspoon salt
dash of pepper

Put the cleaned singed duck in a deep bowl. Sprinkle with aniseed and 1 tablespoon coriander; cover with water. Let stand at least 2 hours. Remove from water and drain. To make the stuffing, cook chopped onion and ground beef in melted butter till slightly browned. Stir in raisins, coriander, salt, and pepper. Spoon stuffing into duck cavity and sew or skewer the opening together. Insert spit through center of bird and roast in preheated broiler rotisserie 2 to 2 1/2 hours, or until tender. To roast in oven, prepare as above. Roast uncovered in 325° F. oven.

ROAST MALLARD DUCK

Remove all strong flavors from bird by placing in cold water and adding 2 tablespoons salt for each quart of water; allow to stand overnight, then dry thoroughly inside and out. Season cavity with salt, pepper and celery salt. Put chunks of apples, onions and celery inside to fill bird. Place thin strips of bacon around breast and tie. In a roaster with a cover, place duck breast down; pour about 2 inches of water into pan so that breast of bird will be lying in water. Cover. Bake in 350°F. oven 3 1/2 hours, or until bird is tender. Remove roaster from oven and remove 1/2 of remaining liquid. Turn duck breast side up and roast, uncovered, at 400°F. about 25 minutes or until breast is browned. Keep bacon on breast, and baste occasionally while it is browning. Serves 2.

SPORTSMAN'S DELIGHT

Prepare wild duck for roasting. Chop 1 small onion fine and add to 2 cups drained sauerkraut along with 1 teaspoon caraway seed. Stuff duck with this mixture and roast in 350°F. oven, basting several times with butter during the roasting. Serves 2.

BRAISED WILD DUCK

1 duck, cut in serving pieces
2 onions, diced
3 tablespoons flour
3/4 cup beer
1/2 cup chicken stock
1/8 teaspoon thyme
1/8 teaspoon basil

Brown the meat in a little fat. Brown the onions. Add the flour. Stir in the beer, stock, thyme, and basil. Add browned duck pieces. Cover and cook over low heat 1 hour or until duck is tender. Skim off fat. Serves 4.

ROAST DUCK WITH APPLE STUFFING

2 large mallards
1/2 cup chopped celery
1/2 cup chopped onion
2 medium apples, cut up
1/4 cup brown sugar
1/4 cup chopped walnuts
2 to 4 slices bread, cubed
1/4 cup raisins
dash of pepper
1/8 teaspoon marjoram
dash of sage
1/2 teaspoon salt
1 bouillon cube
1 cup warm water

Soak ducks overnight in salt and water brine. Drain; place in roasting pan. Mix celery, onion, apples, brown sugar, walnuts, bread cubes, raisins and seasonings. Dissolve bouillon cube in 1 cup warm water; add 1/2 cup bouillon to dressing mixture to moisten. Place dressing around ducks. Pour remaining bouillon over ducks. Bake in 325°F. oven 1 hour and 30 minutes or until done. Serves 4.

SWEET AND SOUR DUCK

5 pounds duck pieces
2 tablespoons fat
2 cups sauerkraut
1 6-ounce can orange juice
concentrate
1/4 cup water
1/2 teaspoon caraway seed

Melt fat in large, heavy skillet and brown all pieces of duck. Scatter sauerkraut over duck. Combine orange juice, water and caraway seed, and pour over sauerkraut. Cover skillet and simmer gently until duck is tender, about 1 1/4 hours. Serves 4 to 6.

Serve this duck with fluffy mashed potatoes and a green vegetable.

DUCK LEG PIE

4 large duck legs
1 teaspoon salt
1 bay leaf
2 stalks celery
2 small onions
1 cup drained canned tomatoes
1/2 cup diced carrots
1/2 cup diced celery
2 cups chopped onion
3 tablespoons flour
6 drops tabasco sauce
1 tablespoon prepared horseradish
1 cup diced cooked potato
1 4-ounce can mushrooms
1 recipe baking powder biscuits

Place duck legs in pot, cover with water. Add 1 teaspoon salt, bay leaf, 2 stalks celery and whole onions. Simmer until meat falls from bones. Put meat in casserole with tomatoes, diced carrots, celery, chopped onion. Thicken 3 cups of the duck stock with 3 tablespoons flour; season with tabasco, horse-radish, salt and pepper to taste. Add to casserole; bake in 350°F. oven 45 minutes. Add potatoes, mushrooms, bake 30 minutes longer. Arrange baking powder biscuits over top; raise oven temperature to 400°F. and bake until biscuits are done. Serves 4.

WILD GEESE

It is generally better to pluck geese, as well as most other birds to be roasted; when skinned, some of the flavor is lost with the skin, and the meat may be dry when cooked. Cut the throat of the goose as soon as you get to where it has fallen, making sure you cut the big vein in the neck. Allow the goose to bleed out completely. This bleeding will insure a much better bird for the table. Follow the method of plucking and drawing given for ducks (page 51). Because of their size, the coating of melted paraffin may be poured over the geese in-stead of dipping—and, of course, a larger amount of paraffin will be needed. Dress the geese in the same manner as ducks. See page 168 for packing and shipping information.

ROAST WILD GOOSE

Quarter 1 large peeled onion and 2 medium unpeeled apples and place in cavity of goose. Spread soft butter over breast. Salt and pepper to taste. Place 4 slices thick-sliced bacon over breast of goose. Place in roasting pan, breast up; add 1 cup sauterne. Cover roaster and bake in 275°F. oven 2 hours. Remove cover and continue to cook at same temperature until brown and tender. Serves 6.

SAVORY STUFFED WILD GOOSE

1 wild goose
juice of 1 lemon
salt, pepper
1/4 cup butter
1/4 cup chopped onion
1 cup chopped apple
1 cup chopped dried apricots
3 cups soft breadcrumbs
1/2 teaspoon salt
1/4 teaspoon pepper
melted fat OR drippings
4 to 6 slices bacon

Rub cleaned goose inside and out with lemon juice and seasonings. For stuffing, melt butter in heavy skillet. Sauté onion until soft and clear; mix in apple, apricots, crumbs, salt and pepper. Spoon stuffing lightly into cavity. Close opening with skewers and string and cover bird with cheesecloth soaked in melted fat. Place breast up in roasting pan. Place bacon slices over bird. Roast in 325°F. oven allowing 20 to 25 minutes per pound, until tender. Baste frequently with fat or pan drippings. If age of goose is uncertain, pour 1 cup water into pan and cover last hour of cooking. Remove cheesecloth, skewers and string before serving. Serves 6.

WILD GOOSE AU FEU

1 medium goose
4 to 5 quarts cold water
1 1/4 ounces salt
2 pounds lean beef
1 pound beef bones, cracked
1 pound carrots
1 pound turnips
1 pound leeks
garlic
black pepper
bay leaf
thyme
1 cup white wine

Remove skin of goose; wash and dry. Split goose into halves. Using a large vessel with a tight-fitting lid, pour in water and dissolve salt. Add goose halves, beef cut into squares and cracked beef bones. If the water doesn't cover all the meat, add enough water and more salt. Very slowly increase temperature and remove scum from the surface of water repeatedly as it forms before liquid comes to a boil. Allow mixture to boil and add well-scraped carrots, turnips, leeks, and a little garlic. Season lightly with pepper and add a bay leaf and pinch of thyme. Pour in the wine. Cover tightly, reduce heat to barely simmer and cook 4 hours. Remove goose, beef and vegetables, drain well and keep them warm. Remove all bones and bits of bones from soup. On large plates, place some of each vegetable on thick pieces of dry french bread. Pour soup over all. The host then carves the goose and serves it with the beef. Serves 8.

A light cheese, such as neufchâtel, and a thin red wine round out this hearty meal.

GOURMET GOOSE

1 6- to 8-pound goose
3 bulbs garlic
3 medium onions
6 parsnips
6 large carrots
6 large potatoes

Lightly salt cavity of goose, but do not stuff. Coarsely chop giblets and simmer in 1 1/2 cups water while goose cooks. Separate garlic cloves, remove skin and chop with the onions (do not skimp on the garlic). Cover bottom of large roaster with cooking oil. Add chopped garlic and onions, place on burner over medium heat. Brown goose on all sides. While goose is browning, scrub vegetables well and pare, reserving the parings. Cut vegetables into bite-size pieces, putting potatoes in one pan, carrots and parsnips together in another. Cover with water until time to cook. When goose is brown on all sides turn down heat to low and put vegetable peelings over top of goose to steam. You may also add a few celery tops, a little parsley, outside lettuce leaves, etc. This will make the sauce. The goose may also be put in a 300°F. oven for about 2 hours. The cover must be kept on the roaster. About 45 minutes before end of cooking time, put vegetables on to cook over low heat, using 1/2 inch of water in pan. When goose is done, remove from pan and keep warm while making sauce (below). Serves 6 to 8.

Sauce

Using all the vegetable peelings, garlic and onions from the pan, and the undrained giblets, whirl a small amount at a time in a blender. (Skim off fat and use to flavor vegetables, instead of butter.) To this sauce, add salt to taste, 1 teaspoonful each rosemary and thyme, and 1/2 teaspoon sweet basil. Heat and keep very hot until serving time. Pass in separate bowl.

This recipe for goose may also be used very successfully for wild duck. Cranberry bread makes a nice addition to the feast.

FRUIT-STUFFED WILD GOOSE

1 6- to 8-pound wild goose
juice of 1 lemon
salt, pepper
1/4 cup butter
1/4 cup chopped onion
1 cup chopped tart apple
1 cup chopped dried apricots
3 cups soft breadcrumbs (made
from day-old bread)
1/2 teaspoon salt
1/8 teaspoon pepper
4 to 6 slices bacon
melted bacon fat

Sprinkle goose inside and out with lemon juice, salt and pepper. Melt butter in a large saucepan. Add onion and cook until tender. Stir in apple, apricots, breadcrumbs, salt and pepper. Spoon stuffing lightly into cavity. Close opening with skewers and string. Cover breast with bacon slices and cheesecloth soaked in melted bacon fat. Place goose breast up on rack in roasting pan. Roast in 325°F. oven 20 to 25 minutes per pound, or until tender, basting frequently with bacon fat and drippings in pan. If age of goose is uncertain, pour 1 cup water into pan and cover last hour of cooking. Remove cheesecloth, skewers and string. Serves 6 to 8.

Red cabbage and corn fritters make delicious accompaniments.

GOOSE WITH GRAPES IN ORANGE SAUCE

Clean a wild goose and wipe inside and out with a damp cloth; stuff with small seedless grapes. Truss goose, tying legs and wings close to body. Sprinkle with salt and pepper. Roast on a rack in 500°F. oven 30 minutes. Reduce temperature to 300°F., cover pan, and roast 2 to 3 hours, or until a fork slips easily into the breast. Baste frequently with hot chicken stock and pour off excess fat as it accumulates. Uncover for last 30 minutes of roasting. Serve at once with Orange Sauce (below).

Orange Sauce

1 cup brown sugar
2 1/2 tablespoons granulated sugar
1 tablespoon cornstarch
1 tablespoon grated orange rind
1 cup orange juice
2 drops tabasco sauce

Cook over low heat until thick and clean. After removing from heat 1 ounce cointreau may be added, if desired.

HOLIDAY CHRISTMAS GOOSE

1 wild goose
tart apples, peeled, cored, sliced
1 onion
celery tops
3 tablespoons butter
1 teaspoon paprika
1/4 teaspoon salt
1/4 teaspoon pepper
1/8 teaspoon thyme
1/8 teaspoon parsley
1/2 pint dry red wine

Clean goose well. Wipe with salt and pepper. Fill cavity with raw tart apples, onion and celery tops. Sew. Place in foil and add melted butter, paprika, salt, pepper, thyme, parlsey and wine. Completely cover with foil. Roast in 350°F. oven; baste often. When done, remove foil from top and brown. Remove stuffing and serve.

SAUCY APPLE GOOSE

1 wild goose
2 apples
1 can applesauce
3/4 cup currant jelly
1 teaspoon cinnamon
1 teaspoon nutmeg
1/2 cup corn syrup

Place two cooking apples, peeled and sliced, in cavity. Bake in 350°F. oven 20 to 25 minutes per pound.

While baking, baste frequently with a sauce made by heating together applesauce, jelly, cinnamon, syrup and nutmeg. Serve with this sauce as a gravy, separately or over carved bird. Serves 4.

RICE-STUFFED WILD GOOSE

1 10- to 12-pound wild goose
1/4 cup butter
2 cups uncooked rice
1/2 cup chopped onion
1/2 cup chopped celery
2 cups water
2 chicken bouillon cubes
1/2 teaspoon parsley flakes
1 teaspoon salt
1/2 teaspoon thyme
1/2 teaspoon pepper
6 slices bacon

Clean goose. To make stuffing, melt butter in large skillet, add rice, onion and celery. Cook slowly, stirring constantly, until rice is lightly browned. Add water, bouillon cubes, parsley and seasonings. Cover and simmer 20 minutes or until rice is tender (adding more water if rice begins to stick). Set aside to cool. When stuffing is cool enough to handle, fill and truss goose. Place in roasting pan, breast side up. Cover breast with bacon slices and roast 25 minutes per pound, basting occasionally. Serves 15.

GOOSE WITH SOUR CREAM AND MUSHROOMS

1 5- to 8-pound goose
garlic salt
paprika
1 1/2 stalks celery, chopped
1 carrot, chopped
1 1/4 teaspoon salt
1 onion, chopped
4 tablespoons flour
1/2 teaspoon rosemary
1/4 teaspoon thyme
1 cup thick sour cream
1 4-ounce can button mushrooms

Wash goose inside and out. Cut off neck and wing tips. Dry goose with paper towel and season with garlic salt and paprika. Place on rack in shallow pan. Roast, uncovered, in 325°F. oven 1 hour or until browned and fat has cooked off. Meanwhile, simmer giblets, neck and wing tips in water to cover, with chopped celery, carrots and 1 teaspoon salt. Skim 3 tablespoons fat from goose; cook onion in fat until soft and yellow. Stir in 2 tablespoons flour, then blend in liquid from giblets; if necessary, add water to make 1 cup stock. Season with rosemary, thyme and the remaining salt. Stir remaining 2 tablespoons flour into sour cream (this keeps it from curdling). Blend into gravy. Place goose in roasting pan; pour gravy and drained mushrooms over it. Cover and continue roasting another 2 hours. Serves 6.

WATERFOWL GIBLETS WITH MUSHROOMS AND ONIONS

1 pound white onions, peeled
1 pound fresh mushrooms
1 pound giblets (necks, hearts, gizzards)
1/4 cup butter
1 tablespoon lemon juice
salt, pepper

Cook onions in salt water 10 minutes. Drain, except for 1/2 cup liquid. Sauté mushrooms and giblets in butter and lemon juice 15 minutes. Serves 6.

GALLINULE, RAIL

Gallinule do not rank among the most delectable of game birds, but can be delicious when skinned and braised. The rail of the tidal marshlands has many devoted hunters, and can be delicious roasted or braised. Unlike gallinule, rail should be plucked.

ROASTED RAIL

Season rail with salt and pepper, stuff with any desired stuffing. Wrap birds in bacon slices. Roast in 400°F. oven 30 minutes, basting frequently with melted butter. Serve on toast or trenchers.

CHICKEN-FRIED RAIL

Split birds as you would a broiling chicken, season with salt and pepper, dip in beaten egg and then in fine dry crumbs which have been seasoned with a pinch of marjoram. Sauté gently in butter, allowing 15 minutes per side. Serve with wedges of lemon.

GALLINULE ITALIAN STYLE

Brown split birds in butter or drippings, season rather highly with salt and cayenne, cover and simmer slowly 1/2 hour. Add any good tomato-based sauce. Simmer for another 1/2 hour.

CURRIED RAIL

2 or 3 rail
1/4 cup butter
1/2 cup minced onion
1 tablespoon curry powder
1 tablespoon flour
2 cups game bird stock
salt, pepper

Split rail, brown in butter, set aside. Brown onion and curry powder; blend in flour, then stock. Stir until thick and smooth. Season to taste. Add birds to this sauce; cover. Simmer 1/2 hour. Serves 2.

SMALL GAME

The handling of small animals differs from that of game birds in the field and in shipping in several ways. There is no problem of whether to pluck or skin—small game is always skinned, except for that proverbial porcupine baked in an open fire in a coating of mud! There is need for reasonable care in order to keep loose fur from getting onto the meat. A cloth dipped in scalding water will wipe away stray bits of fur from the carcasses of animals.

Generally speaking, small game animals are hunted near home and the problem of shipping them does not arise as often as with game birds. Yet small game animals form a large share of our wild meat, and deserve equal consideration with any other form of game in dressing, shipping and cooking. It is estimated, for example, that one wild rabbit is bagged for every other item of game taken by all American hunters, and that the total weight of rabbits is equal to or greater than that of all other game combined. Squirrels, like rabbit, are nationwide in their distribution and, in spite of their size, form an important part of our wild meat supply.

Small game should be dressed as soon as possible and allowed to cool thoroughly. It should then be hung in a cool place. For information on the shipping and storage of small game, see page 168.

BEAVER

There is plenty of good meat on a beaver—a mature animal may weigh as much as 60 pounds. However, for the best eating, choose a younger, smaller animal, for it will be more tender. Beaver meat is dark, rich and delicious

ROAST BEAVER MICHIGAN

Remove all surface fat from beaver. Cover meat with a solution of 1 teaspoon soda in 1 quart water. Parboil by simmering gently 10 minutes. Drain. Place meat in roaster, sprinkle with salt. Cover with sliced onions and strips of bacon. Roast in 350°F. oven. Beaver is done when meat falls off bones. Serves 4 to 6.

POT ROASTED BEAVER

Remove and discard all fat. Cut beaver in serving pieces and marinate overnight in salt water with 2 bay leaves and 4 cloves. Roll in seasoned flour and brown in butter and bacon drippings. Add small amount of water, cover pan and cook until tender. Serves 4 to 6.

BARBECUED BEAVER

Remove all fat from beaver and cut in serving pieces. Soak 3 or 4 hours in water to which has been added 2 rounded tablespoons salt. Place beaver in large kettle; cover with water, add 1 tablespoon salt. Slowly simmer 1 hour. Remove from kettle and rinse meat. Place in roaster. Pour over Barbecue Sauce (below) and bake, covered, in 200°F. oven 3 hours. Turn every half hour. Serves 4 to 6.

Barbecue Sauce

3 tablespoons butter, melted
1 medium onion, chopped
1 teaspoon salt
1/2 teaspoon garlic salt
1/4 teaspoon paprika
1/4 teaspoon hot pepper sauce
1/4 teaspoon dry mustard
1/4 cup catsup
3 tablespoons worcestershire sauce
3 tablespoons cider vinegar
1 tablespoon celery flakes
1/8 teaspoon thyme
1/4 teaspoon marjoram

Mix first 10 ingredients, pour over meat. Over this scatter celery flakes, thyme and marjoram.

ROAST BEAVER

Remove all fat on surface, soak beaver overnight in 1/4 cup vinegar, water to cover. Wash in cold water, place in roaster. Cut several slits in meat. Sprinkle with salt and pepper. Put strips of fresh salt

71

pork over slits and dust with a little flour. Add about 1/4 cup water to pan, roast with lid on until half done. Add more water if needed. Cut up enough onions, celery and carrots to fill 1 cup. Sprinkle over meat. Finish roasting uncovered. Beaver should be cooked until meat falls off bones. Make gravy by adding flour and water to juices and vegetables in the pan. Serves 4 to 6.

BEAVER-TAIL SOUP

Skin and remove all fat from tails of 2 beaver; cut up tails in small pieces. Soak overnight in water with 2 cups vinegar and 2 tablespoons salt for each quart. Place meat in kettle with 4 quarts boiling water. Add 1/4 teaspoon pepper, 1 1/2 teaspoons salt, 1 bay leaf, 2 cloves garlic, minced, 3 carrots, sliced, 3 stalks celery, 2 small onions. When meat is almost tender add 2 cups egg noodles and 1 small can peas, drained. Serves 4 to 6.

FRIED BEAVER WITH ONIONS

Remove skin and all fat. Soak meat overnight in salted water. Cut in serving pieces and parboil 30 minutes in clear water, to which has been added 3 bay leaves and 4 cloves. Dry beaver pieces and roll in seasoned flour. Fry in equal parts butter and bacon drippings. When

meat is brown, add onions which have been separately fried. Serves 5.

Corn on the cob, butter-roasted in foil, goes well with this.

BEAVER-TAIL ROAST

Marinate beaver tail for 24 hours in mixture of 1 cup red wine, 1 cup water, and 1 large onion, chopped. Dry tail and scrape carefully. Parboil until nearly tender in water to cover, to which has been added 1/2 cup vinegar, 1 teaspoon salt. Dry tail again. Dust with flour, dip into beaten egg, then into cracker crumbs. Pour over 3 tablespoons melted butter. Roast on a rack in 350°F. oven until browned and tender. Serve hot with lemon slices. Serves 2.

RABBIT

Most hunters prefer to dress rabbits immediately after they are shot. Removing entrails and letting blood drain at this time has a two-fold advantage. The immediate draining of blood gives the meat a better quality, and discarding entrails removes the chief cause of spoilage and eliminates the necessity of carrying extra weight around for the rest of the hunting day.

To clean a rabbit, make an incision down the belly from anus to

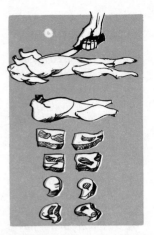

ribs, taking care not to pierce the intestinal casing. The entrails can then be removed all together and blood can be allowed to drain for a few minutes before placing the rabbit in the game pocket of a hunting coat.

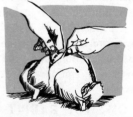

Once you've made the incision, grasp rabbit with one hand at its ears or head and the other at its rump, with the incision directly away from you. Make a quick swing with both arms, and the entrails will leave the carcass as a unit, eliminating the necessity of reaching into the body cavity to re-

move them. The rabbit may also be held by its front feet and given a quick swing to accomplish the same result. The head should be removed and discarded.

The body cavity should be wiped out with a cloth, dry grass, or absorbent paper after entrails have been removed and blood drained. A dozen or more cleansing tissues can be easily carried in a hunting-coat game pocket for this purpose and discarded after use.

Leave skin on rabbit until ready to cook or freeze it. It serves as a protective wrapper and helps to keep meat clean. An ordinary paper bag or two carried in a hunting coat will also serve to keep rabbits clean and to guard game pocket from staining by blood.

A rabbit skin can be removed quickly and easily by making a two-inch cut crosswise through the skin at the middle of the back. Insert first two fingers of each hand into cut. Pull firmly with one hand toward the head, with the other toward the tail. The rabbit skin will come off in two sections in a matter of seconds. Wipe the carcass with a cloth dipped in scalding water to remove loose hair.

Shipping procedure for rabbits is much the same as for game birds. After rabbits have been cleaned, skinned, and frozen, they should be packed surrounded with dry ice

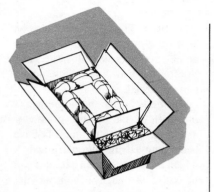

and shipped in a sealed, moisture-proof carton. If the weather is mild or the journey long, one box should be surrounded with a layer of crumpled paper or other insulating material and enclosed in another larger box or carton to get the maximum cooling value of the ice. Rabbits shipped without dry ice should be thoroughly frozen and carefully packaged with a surrounding layer of good insulating material. Prepared this way, they may be shipped for short periods at average fall temperatures.

Some people prefer that rabbit be soaked in vinegar or wine before cooking. Others like them soaked in salted water. Still others prefer to take them as they are, without soaking. Whether or not you choose to soak the rabbit first is a matter of taste.

Regardless of the choice, rabbit, cooked in any number of ways, is a delicious dish.

ITALIAN RABBIT

1 rabbit, cleaned and cut in
serving pieces
red wine
4 tablespoons butter
2 medium onions, sliced
3 tablespoons flour
1 1/2 cups water
1 can mushrooms
1 teaspoon salt
1/4 teaspoon pepper
1 bay leaf
1/2 teaspoon parsley flakes
1/4 teaspoon oregano
1/4 teaspoon thyme

Soak meat overnight in wine to cover. Melt butter in deep skillet, add onions, and sauté until tender. Blend in flour and add 1 cup wine in which rabbit was marinated. Put in water, mushrooms, remaining wine, salt, pepper, bay leaf, parsley flakes, oregano, and thyme. Bring mixture to boil and add meat. Cover and simmer 1 1/2 hours. Serves 4.

SNOWSHOE RABBIT BAKE

Cut rabbit in serving pieces, season. Melt generous amount of butter in large skillet; brown rabbit pieces well. Remove rabbit to a baking pan that can be covered. To butter remaining in skillet add 1/2 teaspoon nutmeg, 1/2 teaspoon cinnamon, 1 teaspoon powdered horseradish (or 2 teaspoons fresh).

Mix and pour over rabbit pieces. Add 1/2 cup water, cover pan and bake in 350°F. oven 1 hour. Mix 1 tablespoon flour with 3 tablespoons cold water. Remove rabbit pieces from pan and add flour-water mixture, stirring well. Simmer a few minutes until gravy is thickened. Serve rabbit with gravy and mashed potatoes. Serves 4 to 6.

BAKED STUFFED RABBIT

4 medium potatoes
2 tablespoons butter
1 teaspoon salt
1/2 teaspoon pepper
1/2 teaspoon crumbled sage leaves
1 cup finely chopped celery
1 rabbit, cleaned
2 large carrots, quartered
salt-pork slices

Cook potatoes and mash with butter. Add salt, pepper, sage and celery. Fill rabbit cavity with this stuffing and sew it up. Fold legs under body and skewer in place. Place rabbit on rack in baking pan with quartered carrots. Fasten salt pork over the back of the rabbit with toothpicks. Bake in 400°F. oven. After 10 minutes, pour a cup of hot water over the meat and continue cooking until tender. Ten minutes before serving, remove salt pork to allow the rabbit to brown. Serve with corn on the cob, calico coleslaw and hot buttermilk biscuits. Serves 4.

DEVILED RABBIT

1 5-pound rabbit, cut in serving
pieces
1/4 cup flour
salt, freshly ground pepper
2 tablespoons salad oil
1/4 cup butter
5 slices bacon, blanched and diced
4 shallots, chopped
1 bouquet garni (garlic clove,
parsley sprigs, bay leaf, tied
in cheesecloth)
2/3 cup dry white wine
2/3 cup chicken broth
2 teaspoons Dijon mustard
2 teaspoons English mustard
1 1/4 cups heavy cream
salt, pepper

Roll rabbit pieces in flour seasoned with salt and pepper. Sauté in the oil and butter with the diced bacon. Add shallots and bouquet garni. Add wine and chicken broth and simmer, covered, until rabbit is tender, 35 to 45 minutes. Remove rabbit to a hot serving platter. Remove bouquet garni and discard. Skim fat from liquid remaining in the pan. Mix the two mustards with the cream and add to the pan drippings. Season with salt and pepper to taste. Simmer 15 minutes. Return rabbit pieces to sauce and heat through. Serves 4.

OREGANO RABBIT

*1 small rabbit, cut in
serving pieces
salt, pepper
1/8 teaspoon crushed oregano
2 tablespoons milk
1 egg
1/4 cup flour
1/2 cup fine dry breadcrumbs*

Sprinkle each rabbit piece with salt, pepper and oregano. Combine milk and egg; beat lightly. Dip seasoned rabbit in flour, then in egg mixture, then in breadcrumbs. Brown on all sides in 1/2 inch of fat heated to 375°. Reduce heat. Cook 20 to 30 minutes longer, or until tender. Drain on absorbent paper. Serves 2 to 3.

Serve this crispy rabbit with corn pudding, waldorf salad and hot biscuits.

HAM-RABBIT PIE

*1 rabbit, cut in serving pieces
rich pie crust
1 pound bacon
2 cups breadcrumbs
salt, pepper
1/2 teaspoon mace
2 tablespoons chopped shallot
2 tablespoons chopped parsley
chicken OR game stock
thin-sliced cooked ham*

Parboil rabbit and rabbit liver

1/2 hour in salted water to cover. Drain. Make pie crust and refrigerate. Cook bacon; drain and crumble. Chop rabbit liver and mix with crumbled bacon, crumbs, seasonings. Moisten with just enough stock to hold together. Place in bottom of baking dish. Lay rabbit pieces on top, then enough slices of ham to cover. Roll out pastry and cover dish, making slashes in pastry for steam to escape. Bake in 450°F. oven 10 minutes; lower temperature to 350° and bake 45 minutes. Serves 6.

STEWED RABBIT

*2 rabbits
salt, pepper
2 medium onions, fine-chopped
3 tablespoons vegetable oil
1-inch cube ham, fine-chopped
1 cup water
1 small can mushrooms
2 tablespoons sherry*

Clean rabbit, cut at joints in serving pieces. Rub each piece with salt and pepper. Brown rabbit and onion in vegetable oil, then add chopped ham, water, mushrooms and wine. Stir well, season again to taste. Simmer 1 hour. Serve hot. Serves 8.

BATTER-FRIED RABBIT

Make a batter of 1 cup sour milk, 1/2 teaspoon baking soda,

1/2 teaspoon salt, 1 egg, 1/2 cup flour. Cut rabbit in small pieces, put in kettle. Season, cover with water, and simmer until tender. Drain, dip pieces in batter and fry in hot lard until brown on all sides.

FRICASSEE OF RABBIT

1 3-pound rabbit
vinegar brine
1 1/2 teaspoons monosodium
glutamate
2 teaspoons salt
1 1/2 teaspoons pepper
1/2 teaspoon saffron
1/4 teaspoon oregano
bacon drippings
1 large onion, chopped
1 tablespoon vinegar
1/2 cup water

Cut rabbit in serving pieces. Let stand in vinegar brine for 3 hours; drain and dry. Sprinkle monosodium glutamate evenly on rabbit pieces. Cover and allow to stand in cool place several hours or overnight. Mix together salt, pepper, saffron and oregano and rub into meat. Heat bacon drippings in deep heavy skillet to depth of 1 inch. Fry rabbit slowly until a rich golden brown on all sides. Place onion in bottom of casserole; arrange rabbit on top of onion. Combine vinegar and water; pour over rabbit. Cover tightly, bake in 275°F. oven 2 hours, or until rabbit is tender. Serves 4 to 6.

JUGGED HARE

3 medium onions, quartered
4 sprigs parsley
2 bay leaves
3/4 teaspoon rosemary
1/4 teaspoon thyme
1/4 teaspoon pepper
2 1/2 cups red wine
1/2 cup red wine vinegar
2 tablespoons salad oil
1 rabbit, cut in serving pieces
flour
10 tablespoons butter
1/2 pound bacon, diced
4 medium carrots, halved
1 3/4 cups beef stock
1/4 cup currant jelly, melted

Prepare marinade by combining 1 onion, 2 sprigs parsley, bay leaves, 1/4 teaspoon rosemary, the thyme and pepper, 1 1/2 cups of wine, the vinegar and the oil. Pour over rabbit; cover and refrigerate 24 hours, turning occasionally. Drain, reserving marinade. Dredge rabbit with flour. In a Dutch oven, brown a few pieces at a time in 6 tablespoons of butter. Return meat to pot with bacon, carrots, remaining onion, parsley, rosemary, stock, 1 quart water and 1/2 cup of reserved marinade. Cover and simmer 1 1/2 to 2 hours, or until meat is tender. Remove meat and keep warm. Add jelly and remaining wine to pot. Blend 1 tablespoon flour with remaining marinade and stir into simmering liquid. Serves 4 to 6.

BRAISED RABBIT

Cut meat in serving pieces and soak overnight in water to which a bit of baking soda has been added. Remove, drain and wipe dry. Shake pieces of meat in paper bag containing flour, salt and pepper. Brown rabbit well in bacon fat or other shortening. Place in a roaster, sprinkle with 2 carrots, chopped; add 1 cup water and bake in 300°F. oven until tender.

RABBIT WITH FRUIT GRAVY

1 rabbit
1 cup vinegar
2 parsley roots
2 carrots, sliced
1 stalk celery, sliced
1 teaspoon mixed whole spices
1 teaspoon salt
1 tablespoon butter
1 onion, chopped
1/2 cup raisins
1/2 cup pitted prunes
2 tablespoons flour
2 tablespoons butter

Cut rabbit in serving pieces. Cook next 6 ingredients in 2 quarts water about 10 minutes. Cool and pour over rabbit meat. Marinate 3 days in refrigerator. Remove meat from marinade and brown in 1 tablespoon butter along with 1 chopped onion. Add 1 cup of the brine and 2 cups water and stew until tender. In a separate pan cook raisins and prunes in small amount of water until tender. Strain liquid in which rabbit was cooked and pour back over meat. Add prunes and raisins and their juice. Brown 2 tablespoons flour in 2 tablespoons butter and use to thicken gravy. Serves 2.

This fruited rabbit is delicious served with dumplings.

RABBIT PIE

3 cups cooked rabbit meat
1/4 cup butter
1/2 cup chopped green pepper
1/4 cup chopped onion
1/4 cup sifted flour
2 cups rabbit broth
salt, pepper

Dice rabbit meat coarsely. Heat butter in large frying pan. Add green pepper and onion and cook about 5 minutes. Blend in flour and cook until mixture bubbles. Gradually pour in broth, stirring constantly. Cook until thick and smooth and add salt and pepper.

Add meat to sauce and heat thoroughly. Pour mixture into shallow baking dish or pan and let stand while preparing pastry (below). Serves 6.

Pastry

1 cup sifted flour
1/2 teaspoon salt
1/4 cup shortening
2 tablespoons cold water

Mix flour and salt, cut in shortening, and moisten with water. Roll out the pastry and cut slits to allow steam to escape. Fit pastry to top of dish or pan, crimping edges of crust. Bake pie in 425°F. oven 15 to 20 minutes, or until crust browns and sauce bubbles.

RABBIT WITH HERBS

1 young rabbit, cut in serving pieces
4 tablespoons butter
2 tablespoons fine-chopped parsley
1 tablespoon fine-chopped chives
2 tablespoons flour
1 cup dry white wine
1 cup water
1 large garlic clove, minced
1 teaspoon dried thyme leaves
1 teaspoon salt
1/4 teaspoon pepper
1 3-ounce can sliced mushrooms, drained

In a large heavy skillet, heat 2 tablespoons butter and sauté rabbit until brown on all sides. While rabbit is cooking mix parsley, chives, and remaining 2 tablespoons of butter thoroughly with a fork. Sprinkle rabbit pieces with flour, cook 1 minute, stirring with wooden spoon. Add wine, water, butter-and-herb mixture, garlic, thyme, salt, pepper. Stir over high heat until mixture starts to boil. Cover and simmer 50 minutes over very low heat, then add mushrooms. Simmer 10 minutes more. Serves 4.

SHERRY-BAKED RABBIT

1 3-pound rabbit, cut into pieces
seasoned flour
1/4 cup butter OR bacon drippings
1 cup catsup
1/2 cup sherry
1/3 cup water
2 tablespoons lemon juice
1 medium onion, minced
1 tablespoon worcestershire sauce
2 tablespoons melted butter
1 tablespoon brown sugar

Coat rabbit with seasoned flour. Heat oven to 325°F. Meanwhile, cook rabbit until evenly brown in hot butter or drippings in large skillet. Remove to 2-quart casserole. Combine remaining ingredients in saucepan; bring to boil, and pour over rabbit. Bake covered 1 hour, or until tender. Serves 2 to 3.
Fresh hot biscuits go with this.

BAKED RABBIT MILANESE

1 rabbit
1 tray ice cubes
1 cup red OR white wine
salt, pepper
2 cloves garlic
1 slice lemon
1/2 onion, cut in several pieces
celery leaves
1 tablespoon whole allspice
3 ounces oil
salt pork, sliced thin
4 sage leaves, chopped

Clean and wash rabbit and marinate it for 24 hours in a mixture of next 8 ingredients. Remove rabbit from marinade, cut in serving pieces, and place in roaster with oil. Cover each piece with a thin slice of salt pork, sprinkle with chopped sage leaves, and brown and bake slowly in 300°F. to 325°F. oven about 1 1/2 hours. While rabbit is cooking, make separate sauce (below) in saucepan on range. Serves 3 to 4.

Sauce

4 slices prosciutto
2 slices liver (calves, rabbit,
OR chicken)
1 clove garlic
1 slice lemon
3 ounces butter
salt, pepper
a pinch of red pepper
1/2 cup white wine
1/2 cup water
1 teaspoon tomato paste

Chop first 4 ingredients fine, mix together, and cook in butter. Season with salt and pepper and a pinch of red pepper. Cook slowly 10 minutes. Add the wine, water, and tomato paste and cook 25 minutes. Pour over rabbit which has been baking during this process and bake 10 minutes.

MARINATED RABBIT

1 rabbit
1/2 cup melted butter
1/2 cup salad oil
1/3 cup lemon juice
1/4 cup soy sauce
1 clove minced garlic
1 teaspoon oregano
1 tablespoon chopped parsley
1/2 teaspoon salt
1/4 teaspoon pepper

Cut rabbit into quarters, or smaller pieces if desired. Place in a shallow baking pan and cover with marinade of the above ingredients. Allow to stand overnight at room temperature. When ready to cook, brush the marinade from the meat and place meat on a baking pan in a 375°F. oven for about half an hour, long enough for the rabbit to brown. Reserve marinade, and with a pastry brush, lightly brush it over meat while it continues to cook, using about a quarter of its volume. Allow about 15 minutes in the oven, then baste again at 15-minute intervals, until rabbit is tender. Serves 3 to 4.

RABBIT-POTATO SALAD

2 cups cooked rabbit, coarsely cut
1/4 cup chopped sweet pickles
1/2 cup chopped celery
1 tablespoon chopped onion
1/2 cup diced cooked potatoes
1/2 teaspoon salt
1 tablespoon liquid from
sweet pickles
1/2 tablespoon lemon juice
1/4 cup mayonnaise OR other thick
dressing

Mix first 6 ingredients lightly, but thoroughly. Blend pickle juice, lemon juice, and dressing together, then mix with other ingredients. Chill for about 1 hour to blend flavors. Serves 4.

RABBIT ROASTED WITH CREAM

1 rabbit, cut in serving pieces
several slices bacon
1/2 cup water
1/2 cup wine
1/2 cup vinegar
1 medium onion, sliced
1/2 teaspoon thyme
1 tablespoon mixed spices
1 bay leaf
beef stock
1 cup sour cream

Salt rabbit meat liberally and allow to stand 15 minutes. Rinse, drain, and salt lightly. Put into container along with bacon. Bring water, wine, and vinegar to a boil along with the onion and seasonings. Cool liquid and pour over rabbit. Let stand in a cool place three days. Butter bottom of roasting pan and place drained rabbit and bacon in it. Strain marinade and measure. Mix with an equal amount of beef stock. Then pour half marinade-stock mixture into roaster. Bake in 325°F. oven. When approximately half done, pour part of the cream over rabbit and continue to do so at intervals until cream is used up and rabbit is tender. If desired, make extra gravy with remaining marinade and more cream. Serves 4.

ROAST RABBIT WITH POTATO STUFFING

1 rabbit
2 cups mashed potatoes
2 tablespoons butter, melted
1 teaspoon salt
1/2 teaspoon pepper
1/2 teaspoon poultry seasoning
1 cup minced celery

Mix all together and use to stuff rabbit. Skewer and place in baking pan with legs folded under body. Lay strips of bacon over back of rabbit. Roast in 400°F. oven for 10 minutes; pour 1 1/2 cups hot water over rabbit and bake until done, about 1 hour. Shortly before rabbit is done, remove bacon to allow browning. Serves 2.

OVEN-BRAISED RABBIT

1 5- to 6-pound rabbit, split
salt, pepper
2 tablespoons bacon fat
1 carrot, chopped
1/2 small onion, chopped
1 cup consommé
2 sprigs fresh thyme

Lard hind legs and back of rabbit (or lay strips of salt pork over it while it cooks). Sprinkle rabbit with salt and pepper. Melt bacon fat in heavy skillet; add carrot and onion. Cook 5 minutes. Meanwhile heat consommé with thyme 5 minutes, strain, and reheat. Brown rabbit pieces lightly in bacon fat. Put into baking pan and pour hot consommé around rabbit. Bake in 400°F. oven 45 minutes or until tender, basting four times with pan juices. Serves 4 to 6.

RABBIT BELGIAN STYLE

1 rabbit
2 cups claret wine
1 cup vinegar
1 teaspoon salt
8 whole black peppercorns
1 bay leaf
1/4 teaspoon thyme
1/4 teaspoon marjoram
3 tablespoons salad oil
1/2 pound pitted prunes

Cut rabbit in serving pieces. Then make a marinade of all but the last 2 ingredients and let rabbit stand in it for 24 hours. Drain, reserving marinade. Brown rabbit pieces in 3 tablespoons salad oil in heavy skillet. Add 1 cup of marinade, cover, and simmer for half an hour. Add prunes and continue to simmer until rabbit is tender, adding more marinade if necessary. Thicken gravy and serve. Serves 2.

RABBIT SMOTHERED IN ONIONS

1 3-pound rabbit, cut in
serving pieces
flour
3 large onions, sliced
3 tablespoons shortening
1 cup sour cream
salt, pepper

Dredge rabbit pieces in flour. Then sauté onions in shortening in skillet, remove from skillet, and sauté rabbit in remaining shortening in skillet until brown on all sides. Cover rabbit with the onions; pour sour cream over top of rabbit and onions. Cover and cook slowly for 1 hour on top of stove, or bake in 350°F. oven 35 to 45 minutes. Uncover, bake 15 minutes longer. Season with salt and pepper. Serves 2 to 3.

HARE OR RABBIT SALMI

1 hare OR rabbit
1 slice onion
1 stalk celery, minced
1 bay leaf
2 tablespoons oil
2 tablespoons fat
2 tablespoons flour
2 cups hot water
1 teaspoon salt
1 tablespoon worcestershire sauce
1 tablespoon capers
12 pitted olives
chopped parsley

Clean and dress rabbit. Place in baking pan and add onion, celery, and bay leaf. Brush with oil and roast in 350°F. oven 45 minutes. Remove meat from pan, add fat and flour and stir until sauce becomes rich brown in color. Add hot water, stir well. When smooth, add salt, worcestershire sauce, capers, and olives. Replace meat, cover closely, and roast in 350°F. oven for an additional 80 minutes, or until tender. Arrange rabbit on platter, cover with strained sauce, arrange olives as a garnish, and sprinkle with finely chopped parsley. Serves 6.

RABBIT AND NOODLES

Cook 1 rabbit in salted water, with 1 chopped onion until meat falls from bones. Then dice meat and place in buttered casserole with Noodle Squares (below), covering bottom of casserole with squares first, then adding a layer of meat. Continue process, alternating the layers of noodles and meat until both are used up. Pour the broth in which the rabbit was cooked over the top and bake in 375°F. oven 30 minutes. Serves 3 to 4.

Noodle Squares

2 eggs, lightly beaten
1/4 teaspoon baking powder
1 teaspoon salt
1/2 cup milk
flour

To lightly beaten eggs, add baking powder, salt, and milk. Then add enough flour to form a stiff dough. Roll out on floured board to 1/8-inch thickness. Cut into 1 1/2-inch squares.

CURRIED WILD RABBIT WITH VEGETABLES

3 to 4 pounds of rabbit
1/2 cup flour
2 teaspoons salt
1 1/2 teaspoons curry powder
1/4 teaspoon paprika
fat for frying
1 cup hot water
8 potatoes, peeled and halved
10 carrots, scraped and cut in
   2-inch lengths
1 large onion, sliced
1 bay leaf
1 cup sour cream

Clean and cut up rabbit. Combine dry ingredients in paper bag, add pieces of rabbit, and shake. Remove from bag and brown in fat on all sides. Add water. Cover and simmer for about 1 hour, add vegetables and bay leaf; cook an additional 30 minutes, or until done. Arrange rabbit and vegetables on a hot platter. Add 1 cup sour cream to liquid in pan and thicken for gravy. Serve hot. Serves 8.

HASENBRATEN

Cut 1 rabbit in serving pieces and cook in salted water until tender. Drain and place in shallow baking pan. Mix together: 1 cup thick sour cream, 2 tablespoons flour, 1/2 teaspoon salt, dash of white pepper. Pour over rabbit. Bake in 350°F. oven until golden. Serves 2.

RABBIT PARK AVENUE

1 tender young rabbit, cut in
serving pieces
seasoned flour
butter
1/4 pound salt pork
1 small onion
1 cup cracker OR breadcrumbs
salt, freshly ground pepper
8 to 10 sage leaves, chopped,
OR 1 teaspoon dry sage
1 egg, beaten
butter OR salt-pork cubes

Shake the rabbit pieces in bag of seasoned flour, then brown in butter and set aside. Run salt pork and onion through food chopper. Add breadcrumbs, salt and pepper, and sage. Stir in egg and pour mixture into baking dish spreading it evenly across bottom. Arrange rabbit meat on top, dot with butter or salt pork cubes, and bake in 350°F. oven about 45 minutes, or until tender. Serves 2 to 4.

RABBIT MARSHFIELD STEW

1 small rabbit, cut in serving pieces
2 cups dried lima beans
2 teaspoons salt
1/8 teaspoon pepper
1 teaspoon monosodium glutamate
1 bay leaf
1 medium onion, sliced
1 bunch carrots, sliced
2 large green peppers
2 tablespoons butter OR margarine

Wash rabbit; place in large kettle with drained beans which have been soaked overnight in 1 1/2 quarts of cold water. Cover with boiling water and add salt, pepper, monosodium glutamate, bay leaf, and onion. Simmer half an hour. Add carrots and cook 1 hour longer, or until rabbit is tender, adding more boiling water as needed. Cut seeded green peppers in rings. Add during last 15 minutes with butter or margarine. Serves 6.

RABBIT FRICASSEED IN BEER

1 rabbit, cut in serving pieces
salt, pepper
flour
1/2 cup butter
2 tablespoons flour
1 3- or 4-ounce can mushrooms
3/4 cup beer
1 8-ounce can white onions, drained
1 cup cooked French style
green beans

Sprinkle rabbit with salt and pepper and roll in flour. Melt butter in a large skillet, add meat, and brown on all sides. Remove from pan. Blend 2 tablespoons flour into remaining fat. Drain juice from canned mushrooms and add enough water to it to make 1 1/4 cups liquid, placing mushrooms aside. Gradually stir liquid mixture into skillet and cook, stirring constantly until thickened. Stir in beer. Return rabbit to skillet, cover, and simmer about 1 hour, or until tender. Add mushrooms, onions, and green beans, and simmer until heated through. Serves 4.

Crusty bread goes well with this.

OLD-FASHIONED FRICASSEED RABBIT

Cut rabbit in serving pieces, place in stewing pot, and season with 1/2 teaspoon salt, few grains cayenne, 1/4 cup chopped parsley. Pour in 2 cups warm water or veal broth, and simmer until rabbit is tender. Remove rabbit pieces and keep warm. Add several small pieces of butter rolled in flour to pot and simmer until gravy is thickened. Just before turning off heat, enrich with 1 cup heavy cream. Serves 3 to 4.

So that wonderful gravy won't go to waste, serve on crispy biscuits.

RABBIT RAGOUT WITH DUMPLINGS

1 1/2 pounds rabbit meat
1/2 cup flour
1 teaspoon salt
1/2 teaspoon pepper
3 tablespoons fat
4 potatoes, diced
4 carrots, sliced
2 onions, diced
1 tablespoon parsley
flour
water

Cut rabbit meat into 1-inch cubes. Mix flour, salt, and pepper together and dust meat with mixture. Melt fat in large kettle, add meat, and brown. Add enough hot water to cover meat, cover kettle, and simmer 2 hours, or until meat is tender. Add vegetables and cook an additional half hour. Thicken stew with 1 1/2 tablespoons flour and water. Once gravy is thick enough, drop in dumpling-batter by spoonsful to make dumplings (below). Cover kettle tightly and boil gently for 15 minutes. Serve gravy, meat and vegetables, sprinkled with parsley. Serves 3 to 4.

Dumplings

1 cup sifted flour
2 teaspoons baking powder
1/2 teaspoon salt
1 egg
1/2 cup milk

Mix and sift the dry ingredients together. Beat egg, add milk, and finally add the flour mixture. Mix lightly.

HONEYED RABBIT

1 rabbit
1 medium onion, sliced
1 clove garlic, fine-chopped
1 tablespoon parsley, chopped
3 tablespoons cooking oil
3 1/2 cups tomato juice and pulp
1/2 teaspoon salt
1/4 cup milk
1/4 cup honey
1 cup sifted flour
1/4 teaspoon pepper
1 teaspoon salt
6 tablespoons cooking oil

Sauté onion, garlic, parsley in oil until onion is golden brown. Strain tomato pulp from juice and add pulp and 1/2 teaspoon salt to

pan. Simmer 10 minutes. Mix in milk and honey. Dip rabbit in mixture, then roll in flour seasoned with salt and pepper. Brown in oil. Cover with sauce and tomato juice and simmer about 1 1/2 hours. Serves 3 to 4.

RABBIT CASSEROLE

1 young rabbit, cut in serving pieces
1/4 cup flour
1 teaspoon salt
1/4 teaspoon pepper
1/4 teaspoon marjoram
1/2 teaspoon monosodium glutamate
6 slices bacon, cut in squares
4 medium potatoes, pared and sliced thin
2 small onions, sliced
2 bouillon cubes
2 1/2 cups hot water

Dip rabbit pieces in a mixture of flour, salt and pepper, marjoram, and monosodium glutamate, and let stand for a moment. Fry bacon slowly until lightly brown, then remove from pan and pour off half the fat. Brown rabbit in remaining bacon fat, then transfer to casserole. Cover with potato and onion slices. Sprinkle lightly with remaining seasoned flour. Dissolve bouillon cubes in hot water and add to casserole. Cover and cook in 350°F. oven 2 hours. Remove cover for 15 minutes to brown. Serve with bacon. Serves 4 to 5.

MOLDED RABBIT

1 rabbit
1/2 pound ham
pepper, salt
3/4 ounce gelatin

Joint and wash rabbit, put in stewing pan with the ham, seasonings, and sufficient water to cover. Simmer until tender. Lift rabbit out, remove bones, and cut rabbit meat and ham into small pieces. Dissolve gelatin in the stock (1 pint) in which rabbit and ham were cooked. Add the two meats and cook 5 minutes. Pour into a wet mold. When cold, turn out and garnish with salad greens, tomatoes. Serves 3 to 4.

LOUISIANA RABBIT

2 to 3 pounds tender young rabbit
1/2 cup flour
1 1/2 teaspoons salt
1/4 teaspoon pepper
1/4 cup butter or oil
2 medium onions, sliced
1 clove garlic, minced
1 tablespoon chopped parsley
3 tablespoons butter or oil
3 1/2 cups tomato juice
1/4 teaspoon Worcestershire sauce
Salt and pepper to taste

Shake moist pieces of rabbit in plastic bag in mixture of flour, salt, and pepper. In heavy skillet heat fat and brown rabbit lightly on all sides. Meantime, cook onions, garlic, and parsley in fat until onion is golden brown. Add tomato juice and Worcestershire sauce and simmer for 15 minutes. Season to taste. Transfer rabbit to casserole dish; pour sauce over rabbit, cover and bake 1 hour in a 325°F. oven or until tender. Uncover and bake 30 minutes to brown top. Serves 4 to 6.

Serve this delicious rabbit dish with brown rice, home-spiced peaches, corn dodgers, endive salad, and top it off with cottage pudding with lemon sauce for dessert.

RABBIT PAPRIKA

1 rabbit
1/4 stick butter
1/4 cup cooking oil
1 medium onion, chopped
1 tablespoon paprika
salt, pepper
water OR chicken broth
1/2 cup sour cream, or more

Sauté rabbit in butter and oil until brown; add onions and sauté them until soft. Add paprika, salt and pepper to taste, and 1/2 cup water or broth. Simmer, and as liquid cooks down, add a little to it now and then until rabbit is done, and only a few tablespoons of liquid remain. Add sour cream and bring to simmer. Serve with buttered noodles. Serves 3 to 4.

This recipe is equally delicious when pheasant is used.

RABBIT PIE WITH BUTTERMILK CRUST

1 rabbit, cooked
3 medium potatoes, diced
1 medium onion, sliced
4 carrots, diced
1/2 package frozen peas
1 small can green beans, drained
2 cans beef OR chicken gravy

Remove meat from bones and dice. Season potatoes, onion, and carrots and cook together until almost done. Add peas, finish cooking, drain off all but 2 tablespoons liquid. Add beans and rabbit to vegetables and stir in gravy. Put in baking dish. Top with Buttermilk Crust (below). Bake in 350°F. oven until brown, about 30 minutes. Serves 4 to 5.

Buttermilk Crust

2 cups sifted all-purpose flour
1/2 teaspoon baking soda
3/4 teaspoon salt
1/3 cup shortening
3/4 cup buttermilk

Mix dry ingredients together, cut in shortening, add buttermilk, and mix well. Pat out to size of baking pan.

RABBIT SALAD

3 cups cold, diced rabbit
2 cups celery, chopped
1 can peas, drained
1 cup mayonnaise
1/4 cup vinegar

Mix first 3 ingredients together. Mix mayonnaise and vinegar and pour over. Mix well. Put in covered bowl and chill in refrigerator for about 3 hours. Serve as a main dish on lettuce. Serves 6.

CODDLED RABBIT

1 rabbit, dressed
1/2 cup vinegar
1/2 cup water
1/4 cup flour
1/2 teaspoon salt
1/8 teaspoon pepper
4 tablespoons butter
4 slices bacon, diced
1 tablespoon parsley, minced
2 onions, fine-chopped
1 cup milk, scalded

Cut rabbit in pieces and marinate for 2 hours in vinegar and water. Remove rabbit, dry and roll in flour seasoned with salt and pepper. Melt butter in hot frying pan and brown rabbit pieces. Arrange in casserole. Add bacon, parsley, onions, and scalded milk. Cover and bake 1 hour, or until tender, in a 300°F. oven. Serves 4.

SWEET-SOUR RABBIT

1 rabbit, cut in serving pieces
flour
salt, pepper
2 tablespoons cooking fat
1 cup pineapple juice
1/4 cup vinegar
1 cup pineapple chunks
1 medium green pepper, diced
1 1/2 tablespoons cornstarch
1/4 cup sugar
1/2 cup water

Dredge rabbit in mixture of flour and salt and pepper. Brown in fat in heavy skillet over moderate heat. Add pineapple juice, vinegar, and 1/2 teaspoon salt. Cover and cook over low heat 40 minutes, or until meat is tender. Add pineapple chunks and green pepper and cook a few minutes longer. Mix cornstarch with sugar and stir in water. Add gradually to pineapple mixture. Cook 5 minutes. Serves 6.

WISCONSIN STYLE RABBIT

1 rabbit, cut in serving pieces
1 cup olive OR salad oil
1 clove garlic, halved
1 cup flour
2 tablespoons dry mustard
1 teaspoon curry powder
1 teaspoon powdered thyme
2 teaspoons salt
1/2 teaspoon pepper
1 cup light cream

Rub rabbit pieces with oil and let stand in a cool place overnight. Rub rabbit with garlic. Combine flour, mustard, curry powder, thyme, salt, and pepper in paper bag, and shake pieces of rabbit in bag until well coated. Fry in remaining oil until golden brown. Reduce heat to simmer. Add cream. Cover and simmer 1 hour, or until tender. Serve on hot platter, pouring cream sauce over rabbit. Serves 5.

RABBIT CREOLE

1 rabbit, cut in serving pieces
1 medium onion, sliced
1 clove garlic, fine-chopped
1 tablespoon chopped parsley
3 tablespoons shortening, melted
3 1/2 cups tomato juice and pulp
1/2 teaspoon salt
1/2 cup milk
1 cup sifted flour
1 teaspoon salt
1/4 teaspoon pepper
4 to 6 tablespoons shortening OR
drippings
green pepper rings
corn relish

Sauté onion, garlic, and parsley in melted shortening in heavy skillet until onion is golden brown. Strain tomato pulp from juice. Add tomato pulp and salt to browned onion, garlic and parsley. Simmer very gently while preparing rabbit. Dip rabbit into milk, then roll in flour, seasoned with salt and pepper. Brown floured pieces in melted shortening or drippings. When browned, cover rabbit with tomato sauce; slowly add strained tomato juice, and simmer gently until rabbit is tender—1 to 1 1/2 hours. Garnish with green pepper rings filled with corn relish. Serves 3 to 4.

BRAISED RABBIT WITH MILK GRAVY

*1 2- to 2 1/2-pound rabbit, cut
in serving pieces
flour
salt, pepper
monosodium glutamate
3 tablespoons cooking fat OR butter
1/2 cup water
1 onion, diced
2 tablespoons flour
2 cups milk*

Roll rabbit in mixture of flour, salt and pepper, and monosodium glutamate. Heat fat in heavy pan and brown rabbit over low heat. Add water and onion and cover pan tightly. Reduce heat and cook slowly until tender, adding more water as needed. Remove rabbit from pan and keep it hot while you stir 2 tablespoons flour into pan. Cook until bubbling. Add milk slowly, stirring occasionally. Taste and season. Serve over rabbit. Serves 3 to 4.

ONE-DISH RABBIT

*1 rabbit, cut in serving pieces
salt, pepper
flour
oil
2 medium onions, sliced 1/2-inch
thick
4 or 5 small potatoes, quartered
1 can tomatoes*

Sprinkle rabbit with salt and pepper and flour. Fry in oil till lightly browned. Layer rabbit, onions, potatoes in casserole. Cover with tomatoes. Bake in 350°F. oven 2 hours. Serve on hot biscuits. Serves 4 to 6.

BEER HASENPFEFFER

*1 large rabbit, cut in
serving portions
1 cup vinegar
1 12-ounce can of beer
2 large onions, sliced
1 tablespoon mixed pickling spices
1 teaspoon salt
1/8 teaspoon pepper
1/4 cup flour
1/2 cup fat
1 tablespoon sugar*

Combine vinegar, beer, onions, pickling spices, and salt and pepper in large earthenware bowl. Add the meat, cover, and let stand in a refrigerator 1 or 2 days, turning the meat several times during that period. Dry the meat with a cloth or absorbent paper and dip it in flour. Melt fat in large skillet and brown meat on all sides. Pour off fat. Strain marinade and add to meat in the skillet with the sugar. Bring liquid to a boil. Reduce heat, cover, and simmer 40 minutes, or until meat is tender. Thicken the liquid with flour mixed with water, if desired. Serves 3 to 4.

Serve with potato dumplings, buttered green beans, and green salad.

DEEP-DISH RABBIT

1 rabbit
1 tablespoon salt
flour
1/4 pound thinly sliced bacon
1 dozen cloves
1 onion
salt, pepper
3 stalks celery
1 small can mushrooms
4 tablespoons flour

Prepare and disjoint rabbit. Let stand 1 hour in cold water containing 1 tablespoon salt. Drain and dry with a soft cloth. Turn each piece of rabbit lightly in flour. Fry bacon in a heavy pan to a golden brown, but not crisp. Remove bacon to a plate and sauté the pieces of rabbit in the hot bacon fat to a medium brown on both sides. Lift fried rabbit to a saucepan. Stick cloves into onion, tie celery into a small bunch, and place in saucepan with the rabbit meat. Pour 1 quart of water into pan in which rabbit was fried. Boil and stir a few minutes, to loosen browned bits on the bottom. Pour through a strainer over rabbit. Simmer rabbit, covered, until tender, about 1 1/2 hours. Then remove onion and celery. Add mushrooms. Taste and season if necessary. Stir flour which has been blended with cold water into boiling gravy until gravy boils and thickens. Lift rabbit to a hot, deep dish, pour gravy through a strainer over rabbit. Reheat bacon in a small pan and serve with rabbit. Serves 4.

ENGLISH RABBIT PIE

1 rabbit
1/2 teaspoon whole black pepper
2 bay leaves
1 small carrot, chopped
2 large onions, chopped
3 stalks celery, diced
salt, pepper

Cut rabbit into serving portions and let stand in cold water 12 hours. Transfer drained rabbit to saucepan, cover with cold water, bring to boiling point, and boil 5 minutes. Drain. Cover with clean hot water again and add the whole black pepper, bay leaves, chopped carrot, onions, celery, and salt and pepper. Simmer 45 minutes, or until tender. Then remove rabbit, place in a deep dish, drain the stock from the saucepan, and strain it. Make a sauce (below), pour over rabbit in deep dish, cover with pie crust. Bake 20 minutes in 375°F. oven. Serves 4.

Sauce

1/2 pound butter
1 cup flour
strained stock
cream
salt pork, cooked and diced
10 small onions, boiled
1 cup boiled diced potatoes,
worcestershire sauce

Blend butter and flour together in saucepan, letting it simmer about 10 minutes. Then add strained stock and cook slowly for 1 hour. Strain and add enough cream to make it white, the diced cooked salt pork, boiled onions, and boiled potatoes, diced. Mix with a dash of worcestershire.

Rabbit stew may be made in same way without using the pie crust.

RABBIT A LA ROCHELLE

3-pound rabbit, cleaned and dressed
brandy
seasoned flour
2 tablespoons bacon drippings
1 cup fresh orange juice
1/4 cup fresh lime juice
1/2 teaspoon salt

Rub dressed rabbit, cut into serving pieces, with cloth saturated with brandy. Then place meat pieces in a bag containing seasoned flour, shake well, and remove. Heat bacon drippings in skillet and sauté rabbit pieces over medium heat, turning until all sides are golden brown. Add the orange juice, lime juice and salt; cover, and simmer over low heat 40 minutes, or until rabbit is tender. Remove meat (only) to hot platter and keep warm while sauce (below) is made. Then pour sauce over rabbit pieces. Serves 4.

Sauce

1 1/2 teaspoons cornstarch
2 ounces cointreau
1/2 cup dry white wine
1 medium green pepper, cut in
thin strips
1 cup canned mandarin orange
sections, drained and halved

Mix first 3 ingredients together and add to skillet with other juices. Blend in green pepper, cut in thin strips, and drained mandarin orange segments, each segment halved. Cook over low heat about 5 minutes.

FRENCH-FRIED RABBIT

Parboil 1 rabbit, cleaned, washed, dried, and cut into serving pieces, for 45 minutes in salted water with 1 medium-size onion, sliced. Remove pieces and drain well on paper towel. Mix 2 tablespoons flour, 1/2 cup condensed milk, and 2 beaten eggs together, and let stand. With rolling pin, roll 1/2 box of crackers into crumbs on waxpaper. Dip each piece of rabbit into egg mixture and roll well in cracker crumbs. Then fry until golden brown in deep fat. Serves 3.

GEORGIA RABBIT STEW

2 rabbits
6 tablespoons hot fat
3 medium onions, cut fine
2 garlic cloves, minced
1/2 cup diced celery
2 tablespoons flour
1/2 cup water
1/2 cup pear juice
1/2 cup pineapple juice
1 teaspoon salt
1/2 teaspoon pepper
1/4 teaspoon thyme
2 4-ounce cans mushrooms

Cut 2 young rabbits in serving pieces and brown quickly in dutch oven in hot fat. Remove meat, and in remaining fat, sauté onions, garlic cloves, and celery until tender. Blend in flour and add water, pear and pineapple juice, salt, pepper, thyme, and the mushrooms, including liquid. Bring mixture to a boil, then simmer several minutes. Return rabbit meat to kettle, cover, and simmer 30 to 40 minutes. Serves 4 to 6.

RABBIT HAMBURG STYLE

1 rabbit
1 sliced onion
1 chopped green pepper
1 cup vinegar
3 tablespoons olive oil
2 tablespoons butter
2 tablespoons browned flour
2 cups beef broth
2 tablespoons sherry
pepper, salt

Cut rabbit in 6 pieces. Place in a deep dish, add next 4 ingredients, and let stand overnight. Melt butter in skillet and brown rabbit. Add browned flour and beef broth and simmer 1 1/2 hours. Cool, skim off fat, and add sherry wine. Season rabbit to taste and heat thoroughly. Serves 3.

OPOSSUM, WOODCHUCK

These animals should be handled in accordance with the general rules for game in the field. The blood should be drained, entrails removed and body cavity wiped clean. When hung for 48 hours they are ready to be skinned and cooked.

Opossum meat is light-colored and tender. Excess fat may be removed, but it contains no strong flavor or odor.

Woodchuck meat is dark and

tender. The excess fat should be removed, but it has no objectionable flavor. With both opossum and woodchuck, it is usual to parboil all but the young animals before roasting or frying.

ROAST OPOSSUM

1 opossum, skinned and cleaned
1 teaspoon each: salt, pepper
1 onion, chopped
1 teaspoon fat
1 opossum liver, chopped
1 cup breadcrumbs
1/4 teaspoon worcestershire sauce
1 hard-cooked egg, chopped
salt, pepper
4 strips bacon

Rub opossum with salt and pepper. Brown onion in fat, add opossum liver and cook until tender. Add breadcrumbs, worcestershire sauce, egg, seasonings and water to moisten. Stuff opossum with this mixture and truss. Place in pan belly down. Put bacon strips across back. Add 1 quart water to pan. Roast uncovered in 350°F. oven until tender, basting every 15 minutes. It will be done in about 2 1/2 hours. Serves 2 to 4.

GLAZED OPOSSUM

Stuff cleaned opossum with any flavored dressing; brush with melted butter. Roast uncovered in 350°F. oven about 2 1/4 hours, basting often with more melted butter and sprinkling opossum with a small amount of brown sugar after each basting. About half an hour before opossum is done, surround with cooked, halved sweet potatoes; sprinkle potatoes heavily with brown sugar and dot with butter. Serves 3.

OPOSSUM AND SWEET POTATOES

1 opossum (about 2 1/2 pounds)
2 1/2 teaspoons salt
black pepper to taste
flour
1/2 cup water
4 medium sweet potatoes or yams
1/4 teaspoon salt
2 tablespoons sugar

Trim excess fat from opossum and discard. Wipe with damp cloth, pick off any clinging hair, then wash quickly inside and out with warm water. Drain thoroughly. Rub salt mixed with pepper well into the opossum inside and out. Sprinkle inside and out with flour. Lay the opossum on its back in a roasting pan with a tight-fitting cover. Add water, cover and bake in 350°F. oven until about half done—from 3/4 to 1 hour, time depending on age of animal. Split peeled potatoes in half lengthwise and place in pan around opossum. Add more water if needed. Cover and cook about 20 minutes longer. Remove cover and sprinkle the potatoes with 1/4 teaspoon salt and the sugar. Continue cooking uncovered until both potatoes and opossum are a luscious brown and tender. Serves 3 to 4.

Hubbard squash baked with the opossum is equally as good as potatoes. Additional butter or other shortening may be used to brown or baste the meat as it cooks.

APPLE-ROASTED OPOSSUM

Parboil a young, cleaned opossum until nearly tender in salted water. Stuff with any favorite dressing. Place opossum on rack in roaster, cover with strips of bacon. Into bottom of roaster pour 3 cups water in which have been dissolved 1 tablespoon each sugar and lemon juice. Bake in 350°F. oven about 2 hours. Drain all but about 1 cup liquid from pan. Surround opossum with pared, quartered apples; sprinkle apples with mixture of 1 cup brown sugar, 1 teaspoon grated lemon rind, 1 teaspoon cinnamon. Continue roasting for half an hour, or until opossum is tender. Serves 3 to 4.

WOODCHUCK BARBECUE BURGERS

1 woodchuck
1/2 cup fresh bread crumbs

1/4 cup ground onion
1 teaspoon salt
1/8 teaspoon pepper
2 eggs
1 tablespoon melted butter
1/2 cup fine, dry bread crumbs
3 tablespoons salad oil
1 cup catsup
1/4 teaspoon Worcestershire sauce

Clean woodchuck. Remove meat from the bones and grind. Add fresh bread crumbs, onion, salt, pepper, one beaten egg and melted butter. Mix thoroughly and shape into patties. Beat remaining egg. Dip patties into egg, then into dry bread crumbs. Fry until brown in hot oil. Mix catsup and Worcestershire sauce and pour over patties. Bake in a 325°F. oven for 1 hour. Serves 6 to 8.

WOODCHUCK IN SAUCE

1 woodchuck
1/2 cup salt
4 mint leaves
1/4 cup oil
1 chopped garlic
salt, black pepper
1/2 cup vinegar
2 cups tomato sauce
pinch of basil

Remove scent glands from chuck. Soak 8 hours in cold water with salt. Cut in 8 pieces and boil 15 minutes. Rinse and repeat soaking process. Rinse again and boil with 4 mint leaves for 45 minutes. Drain and brown with oil and garlic. Salt and pepper both sides. When

95

browned, add 1/2 cup vinegar. Cover and let simmer 8 minutes. Remove from pan and put into pot. Add 2 cups of tomato sauce and a pinch of basil, and cook over moderate heat 1 1/2 hours.

RACCOON, MUSKRAT

Skin the animal, and remove every bit of fat, inside and outside. All layers of fat must be removed. Under the armpits of the front legs, on either side of the spine, and in the small of the back, you will find several small round "kernels" or scent glands. These must be removed to prepare animal for cooking. Both raccoon and muskrat are dark meat and, properly prepared, make tender and flavorful main dishes.

SWEET-SOUR RACCOON

1 raccoon, skinned and cleaned
1 large onion
1 teaspoon dry mustard
1 teaspoon allspice
1 teaspoon salt
1/2 teaspoon pepper
3/4 cup catsup
4 beef bouillon cubes
4 cups water
5 gingersnaps
3/4 cup vinegar
3/4 cup brown sugar

Cut prepared raccoon in serving pieces. Parboil and scrape off all other fat. Place pieces in roasting pan. Add cut-up onion, sprinkle with mustard, allspice, salt and pepper. In separate pan, heat catsup, bouillon cubes, water, gingersnaps, vinegar and brown sugar. Pour over raccoon pieces and roast covered in 350°F. oven until done —about 3 hours. Serves 8.

RACCOON WITH DRESSING

Clean raccoon, removing every bit of fat. Boil until tender with 2 tablespoons salt, 1 tablespoon garlic salt, 1 bunch carrots and 4 stalks celery, cut in chunks, and 4 large sliced onions. When tender, remove raccoon and cut meat from bones. Place in buttered roaster or casserole and cover with Bread Dressing (below). Serves 6 to 8.

Bread Dressing

1 small onion, diced
2 stalks celery, chopped
2 tablespoons powdered sage
1 tablespoon turmeric
4 quarts dry bread, cubed
1 can cream of chicken soup

Mix onion, celery, sage and turmeric with dry bread. Add cream of chicken soup with a little hot water and mix well. If more moisture is needed, add it in the form of hot water. Spread this on top of raccoon, cover and bake in 350°F. oven 20 minutes. Uncover and bake 10 minutes more or until dressing is browned on top.

RACCOON SLOPPY JOE

*1 4- to 6-pound raccoon, cleaned,
    defatted, disjointed
1 medium onion, chopped
1 cup chopped celery
1 tablespoon salt
1/4 teaspoon black pepper
5 cups water
8 to 12 hamburger buns*

Cook all except buns in a covered kettle until meat can easily be removed from bones. Grind in meat grinder or cut in small pieces. Mix with sauce (below); heat thoroughly, spoon into toasted hamburger buns. Serves 8 to 12.

Sauce

*2 medium onions, chopped
1/2 medium green pepper, chopped
2 teaspoons butter OR bacon fat
1 bottle barbecue sauce
1 bottle chili sauce OR catsup*

Sauté onions and green pepper slowly in butter until almost transparent. Add remaining ingredients, and heat. Add raccoon meat and saturate with sauce.

BARBECUED RACCOON

Cut prepared raccoon in serving pieces, place in pressure cooker. Cook at 15 pounds pressure 30 minutes. Let pressure go down normally. Place in baking dish, and pour Barbecue Sauce (below) over meat. Bake in 325°F. oven 1 hour.

Barbecue Sauce

*1/4 cup butter
1/3 cup chopped onion
1 tablespoon flour
1 1/2 cups tomato juice
1/4 cup vinegar
3 tablespoons brown sugar, packed
1 1/2 teaspoons chili powder
1 tablespoon dry mustard
1 tablespoon worcestershire sauce*

Melt butter in large skillet. Add chopped onion and brown lightly; stir in flour. Add other ingredients and simmer 10 minutes.

RACCOON PIE

*1 raccoon
1 quart water
1 pint vinegar
1 tablespoon salt
1 teaspoon pepper
1 tablespoon brown sugar
1/4 ounce pickling spices
1 onion, diced
4 small potatoes
4 small carrots
1 recipe baking powder biscuits*

Cut prepared raccoon in serving pieces. Mix water, vinegar, seasonings, sugar and spices together. Put raccoon pieces in this brine for 8 hours or more. Drain, put in stewing kettle and cover with water. Cook until meat is tender. Add onion, potatoes, carrots. When all ingredients are tender, remove from broth. Thicken liquid with browned flour and butter and season to taste. Place meat and vegetables in a dish and cover with gravy. Cover the top with your own recipe for baking powder biscuits, with a little extra shortening in dough. Cut vent in dough. Bake in 450°F. oven until brown, about 12 to 15 minutes. Serves 8.

ILLINOIS RACCOON SUPPER

3 to 4 raccoons, 4 to 6 pounds each
5 tablespoons salt
2 teaspoons pepper
2 cups flour
1 cup shortening
8 medium onions, peeled
12 small bay leaves

Cut prepared raccoon in serving pieces. Reserve meaty backs and legs for baking. Cook remaining pieces in water to make broth for gravy and dressing. Add small amount of seasonings. Simmer until meat is tender; strain, and use only the broth. Sprinkle back and leg pieces with salt and pepper.

Dredge with flour. Heat shortening in heavy skillet. Add meat; brown on all sides. Transfer pieces to roaster; add onions and bay leaves. Cover. Bake in 350°F. oven 2 hours, or until tender. Make gravy by adding flour to drippings in pan. Use raccoon broth for liquid. Serve pieces over dressing (below), pass gravy. Serves 24.

Dressing

3 loaves day-old bread, crumbled
2 1/2 teaspoons salt
1 teaspoon pepper
2 1/2 teaspoons powdered sage
4 eggs, beaten
1 1 1/2-ounce package dehydrated onion soup
4 stalks celery, chopped
1/2 cup raccoon broth

Bake in large shallow pan in 350°F. oven 30 minutes.

BACON-ROASTED RACCOON

Cut prepared raccoon in serving pieces and soak overnight in salted water. Dry, roll in seasoned flour, brown on all sides in hot fat. Put meat in roasting pan; lay 4 strips or more of bacon over top. Roast in 350°F oven about 3 hours.

RACCOON PATTIES

Cut raccoon meat from bones, grind to make 2 cups. Add 1/2 cup breadcrumbs, 1/4 cup chopped onion, 1/2 teaspoon salt, dash of pepper. Add 1 egg, and mix thoroughly. Form into patties. Dip in beaten egg, then in breadcrumbs. Brown in hot fat. Cover with currant jelly sauce and bake in 300°F. oven 1 hour. Serves 4 to 5.

ROASTED RACCOON WITH GRAVY

1 raccoon, cleaned
beef suet
3 stalks celery
1 large onion
1 teaspoon seasoned salt
1/2 teaspoon pepper

Cut prepared raccoon in serving pieces. Render beef suet in skillet and brown pieces. Place pieces in roaster pan. Cut up celery and onions and add. Sprinkle with seasoned salt and pepper. Cover and roast in 350°F. oven about 3 hours. Gravy (below) can be made from drippings. Serves 8.

Gravy

3 beef bouillon cubes
2 cups hot water
pan drippings
3 tablespoons flour
water

Dissolve cubes in hot water. Add to drippings in pan. Mix flour in a little water until smooth, then stir into mixture. Simmer until it thickens.

STUFFED RACCOON

Wash dressed raccoon in cold water. Parboil by putting meat into cold water, bringing to boil and simmering 20 minutes. Discard water and repeat. Season with salt and pepper and stuff with Chicken Liver Stuffing (below). Roast in 325°F. oven until meat is tender, about 2 hours or a little longer.

Chicken Liver Stuffing

3 tablespoons melted butter
2 chicken livers, chopped
3 tablespoons chopped onion
1 cup chopped celery
4 cups bread cubes
1 egg, lightly beaten
1 teaspoon salt
1/4 teaspoon pepper
1/4 teaspoon sage OR poultry seasoning
milk OR hot water

Melt butter in skillet. Sauté chicken livers until done. Add onion and celery and sauté briefly. Mix with remaining ingredients, using just enough milk or hot water to moisten.

CORN-FRIED RACCOON

1 young raccoon, cut in small pieces
milk
flour
salt, pepper
1/2 cup corn flakes
2 tablespoons bacon drippings

Soak raccoon in milk to cover for 1 hour. Remove. Roll in flour seasoned with salt and pepper. Sprinkle with corn flakes. Fry in hot bacon drippings. For gravy, remove raccoon from pan, drain off most of the fat, stir in flour, brown. Add cold milk, cooking and stirring until heated and thickened. Serves 6.

MOLDED RACCOON SALAD

2 cups chopped cooked raccoon
2 envelopes unflavored gelatin
1/2 cup water
2 cups hot beef bouillon
1/2 teaspoon salt
2 tablespoons chopped onion
1/4 cup lemon juice
1 cup cold water
1/4 tablespoon paprika
3/4 cup salad dressing
1/4 cup sliced stuffed olives
1/4 cup chopped celery
2 tablespoons chopped green pepper

Soften gelatin in water. Add to hot bouillon. Add salt, onion, lemon juice and cold water. Cool until mixture begins to thicken. Mix paprika into salad dressing. Beat salad dressing into gelatin mixture. Fold in raccoon meat, olives, celery and green pepper. Chill until firm. Slice for salad plate or use to make sandwiches. Serves 4.

SAGE-STUFFED RACCOON

Prepare whole raccoon for baking. Rub with generous amount of salt. Stuff with Sage Stuffing (below). Bake in 375°F. oven 2 to 3 hours depending on the size and age of the raccoon.

Sage Stuffing

12 to 14 slices dry bread, cubed
1 1/2 teaspoons ground sage
1 small onion
1 teaspoon salt
1/4 teaspoon pepper
hot water to moisten

Mix all together to a moist consistency. Pack dressing into and around the raccoon.

KRAUT-ROASTED RACCOON

Thoroughly clean raccoon, cut in serving pieces, season with salt and pepper, brown in hot fat. Put browned pieces in roaster and cover with 1 large can sauerkraut. Sprinkle with 1/2 cup brown sugar. Add a little water and bake in

350°F. oven about 3 hours, or until tender.

It's really good. Try this on someone who thinks he doesn't like raccoon— he'll change his mind.

ONION-BAKED RACCOON

1 raccoon
salt, pepper
shortening
4 bay leaves, crumbled
1 package dehydrated onion
soup mix
water

Prepare raccoon and cut in serving pieces. Salt and pepper to taste and brown well in shortening. Place browned pieces in roaster. Add bay leaves and sprinkle dry soup over meat. Add 1 cup water— more may be added during baking. Bake in 325°F. oven until tender.

FRICASSEED RACCOON

Clean game, remove all fat. Cut in serving pieces, rub with salt and pepper. Roll in flour and sauté in hot fat until brown. Add 2 cups water with onion or garlic and 1 bay leaf, cover and simmer 2 hours, or until tender. Remove raccoon and keep warm. Mix 6 tablespoons flour with a little cold water. Add gradually to liquid in which raccoon was cooked, stirring con-

stantly. Simmer 5 minutes. Taste and season. Serve over raccoon, with corn bread.

RACCOON ROAST

Wash raccoon thoroughly in lukewarm water inside and out several times. Parboil about 30 minutes with 1 teaspoon baking soda added to water. Drain, season inside and out with salt and pepper. Then stuff raccoon with Dressing (below). Place in roaster and roast in 375°F. oven, basting often. Drain off fat continually, and add water. Roast approximately 1 1/2 hours or until tender and nicely browned. Before serving, rub roasted raccoon with a cloth soaked in vinegar.

Dressing

3 cups dry breadcrumbs
2 tablespoons melted butter
1 small onion, chopped
1 large sour apple, thin-sliced
1 teaspoon salt
1/4 teaspoon pepper

Combine ingredients, add sufficient water to moisten.

BRAISED RACCOON

Remove all fat from 8 to 10 pounds of raccoon. Cut in serving pieces. Roll in flour and fry in butter until browned on all sides. Put in 5 cans of cream of mushroom soup. Bake in 350°F. oven 2 to 2 1/2 hours, if animal is young; allow more time for older raccoon. Serves 10 to 12.

MARINATED RACCOON, HOT BEEF STYLE

4 raccoon
4 cups vinegar
12 cups water
2 boxes mixed pickling spices
2 large onions, chopped
1 tablespoon salt
1 tablespoon sugar

Take fat off raccoon and cut in half. Place in 5-gallon stone crock. Mix together remaining ingredients and pour over raccoon. Let stand for 48 hours. Bake in roaster in 325°F. oven until meat falls off bones—4 to 5 hours. Cool. Cut meat off bones; dice, and add to Hot Beef-Style Sauce (below). Let simmer in sauce 2 hours. Serves 20.

Hot Beef-Style Sauce

1 can tomato sauce
1/2 cup vinegar
1/2 cup brown sugar
1 large onion
1 tablespoon salt

Put sauce ingredients in electric roaster or large kettle. Mix thoroughly. Simmer 2 hours, add meat.

RACCOON IN SOUR CREAM SAUCE

1 raccoon, trimmed of all fat,
cut in serving pieces
1/2 cup sliced onions
1 teaspoon salt
4 laurel leaves
6 peppercorns
6 whole allspice
1/4 cup vinegar
1 tablespoon flour
1 1/2 cups sour cream

Put raccoon in deep pan, cover with water, add onions, seasonings, vinegar. Simmer until meat is tender. Remove meat, keep hot. Strain stock and return to pan. Stir flour well into sour cream; add to simmering stock, add meat; heat through but do not boil. Serve sauce over meat.

RACCOONBURGERS

Young raccoon should be soaked in salted water 6 hours, old ones 18 to 24 hours. Age meat in refrigerator 1 or 2 days. Strip meat from bones, discarding all fat. For each pound of meat, add:

1 1/2 ounces salt pork
1 6-inch stalk celery
1/2 medium onion
1/2 teaspoon salt
1/2 teaspoon thyme
1/4 teaspoon pepper
1/8 teaspoon cayenne pepper

Put all through a meat grinder twice. Shape into patties and fry or broil, topping with thin slices of American cheese when almost cooked. Allow cheese to melt for about 1 minute. Serve.

RACCOON FEED FOR A CROWD

Soak 1 large raccoon overnight in water to which has been added 3/4 cup vinegar and 4 tablespoons salt. Drain. Simmer raccoon in water to which has been added:

1 clove garlic, crushed
1 bay leaf, crumbled
4 carrots, sliced
4 large stalks celery, sliced
1 teaspoon salt

While raccoon is cooking, cook a 4- to 5-pound pork roast. When meats are done, take from bones and dice. Mix meats together with drippings from pork roast. If necessary, add a little water. Heat, season to taste. Serves 6 to 8.

KRAUT-STUFFED RACCOON

Thoroughly clean raccoon. Salt cavity. Drain 2 quarts fresh sauerkraut and season with salt, pepper and garlic salt. Mix with 2 medium-size cans of mushroom pieces. Stuff raccoon with sauerkraut mixture and roast approximately 3 hours.

BARBECUE-BAKED RACCOON

Remove every bit of fat from raccoon. Parboil it with 1/4 cup salt and 2 or 3 each: onions, potatoes, small rutabaga. When raccoon is tender, cool, remove meat from bones, and dice. Place in baking pan. Mix together:

2 bay leaves, crumbled
1 bottle barbecue sauce
1 can tomato paste
2 tablespoons chili powder
1/2 teaspoon pepper
2 tablespoons celery seed
2 tablespoons brown sugar

Pour over meat and bake in 300°F. oven 1 1/2 hours, adding tomato juice to moisten as needed during the baking.

CAMP-ROAST RACCOON

1 raccoon
2 onions
2 carrots
celery leaves
1 bay leaf
1 teaspoon salt
4 or 5 peppercorns
water for stock
apples; cored, fill with brown sugar

Parboil raccoon; put in kettle with onions, carrots, celery leaves, bay leaf, salt, peppercorns, and enough water to cover. When the water comes to a boil, simmer until raccoon is tender. Remove from kettle and cut away all fat. Reserve stock. Place raccoon in roasting pan; pour 1 cup of the stock over it, and surround with the apples. Bake, uncovered, in 300°F. oven until the meat is crusty brown and the apples cooked.

CURRIED RACCOON

2 young raccoon
3 tablespoons butter
4 tablespoons curry powder
2 cups chicken stock
2 large tomatoes, diced
3 medium onions, fine-chopped
1 tablespoon paprika
1 bay leaf
1-inch piece stick cinnamon
1 tablespoon salt
1 lemon, thin-sliced
1 cup sour cream

Parboil raccoon in salted water to which has been added 1 medium onion, quartered, and 1/4 teaspoon tabasco sauce. Cool raccoon; remove meat from bones and cut in 1-inch cubes. Brown butter in skillet; add curry powder, meat, stir over heat until dark. Add stock, tomatoes, onions, seasonings and lemon; mix well and simmer until meat is tender. Reduce heat and add sour cream. Heat through but do not boil.

Serve this over boiled rice with *side dishes of grated coconut, salted nuts, chutney, raisins, and any other relishes you like. A good substitute for chutney: equal parts India relish, strawberry jam.*

SOUTHERN FRIED MUSKRAT

Wash muskrat, cut in quarters, soak 1 hour or more in well-salted water. Rinse, dry with a cloth, sprinkle with salt and pepper. Beat 2 eggs with 1/2 cup milk. Dip muskrat pieces in flour, then in egg mixture, then in cornmeal. Brown on all sides in hot fat, then lower heat and cook slowly 1 hour. Remove meat and pour off all but 3 tablespoons fat. Add 3 tablespoons flour, stirring rapidly. Slowly add 1 1/2 cups milk and cook until thickened. Season to taste. Serve gravy over muskrat.

Serve this with mashed sweet potatoes, mustard greens and an apple-walnut-celery salad for a wonderful meal.

OVEN-BARBECUED MUSKRAT

If muskrat is old, soak 24 hours in water to which 1 cup vinegar and 2 tablespoons salt have been added for each quart. Drain and dry. Cut in serving pieces. Brown pieces on all sides in hot fat. Place in pan, cover with Barbecue Sauce (below) and bake in 350°F. oven 1 hour or until tender, spooning sauce from pan over meat frequently.

Barbecue Sauce

1/2 cup butter
1 large onion, grated
1/2 cup water
1 tablespoon worcestershire sauce
3 tablespoons lemon juice
1 teaspoon salt
1/2 teaspoon pepper
2 teaspoons paprika
1/2 teaspoon dry mustard
1 tablespoon brown sugar
2 tablespoons tomato paste

Melt butter; add onion and cook until wilted. Add remaining ingredients and simmer 10 minutes.

MUSKRAT CATAWBA

1 large muskrat
salt
water
1 small onion
1/2 teaspoon poultry seasoning
2 eggs
1 cup milk
1 1/4 cups flour
1 teaspoon salt
1/2 teaspoon thyme
1/3 cup shortening

Wipe muskrat with damp cloth. Cut in serving pieces. Put in glass bowl. Add 2 teaspoons salt and 1 quart water. Put in refrigerator overnight. Next day drain and rinse. Put muskrat pieces in kettle, add 1 quart water, 1 1/2 teaspoons salt, onion and poultry seasoning. Heat to boiling, then reduce heat, cover and simmer for 20 minutes. Lift out parboiled meat, drain. Make a smooth batter by beating eggs, milk and flour together, then adding the salt and thyme. Dip pieces of meat in batter. Cook slowly in heated shortening until browned. Add 1/4 cup water, cover and simmer for 20 minutes. Remove cover and cook 15 minutes or until crisp on outside. Serves 8.

BAKED MUSKRAT

Use only hams and shoulders. When skinning animal, take care not to cut into the musk glands on lower belly. Also remove white stringy tissue from inside of each leg. Parboil with 1 sliced onion 30 minutes. Drain, flour the pieces and put in baking dish. Season with salt and pepper, and cover with 8 slices of bacon. Put 1/4 cup vinegar and 1/4 cup water in pan, and roast until tender. Baste frequently with liquor forming in pan. Serves 3 to 4.

SQUIRREL

Squirrel is one of the finest—and one of the tenderest—of all wild meats, having a mild, rarely gamey flavor. There is never any need for soaking, and it takes a mighty tough old squirrel to call for parboiling. The handling of squirrels in the field follows the procedure for rabbits: Clean the squirrels as soon as possible, wipe the body cavity clean with grass, cloth or paper, and allow the body heat to dissipate. Skinning the squirrel can wait until it is prepared for cooking.

BROILED SQUIRREL

Clean squirrels and rub with salt and pepper. Brush with fat and place on hot broiling rack. Broil 40 minutes, turning frequently and basting with drippings every 10 minutes. Serve with lemon wedge.

SAUSAGE-STUFFED SQUIRREL

3 squirrels
1 pound pork sausage
3 tablespoons chopped celery
1/4 teaspoon garlic salt
1 cup toast cubes
1/2 cup cracker crumbs
1/2 teaspoon salt

Cook sausage in skillet, breaking up with fork as it fries. Add celery and garlic salt. Drain off fat. Mix with remaining ingredients and use to stuff squirrels. Sew up squirrels, place on rack in open roaster, and roast in 350°F. oven, basting often, until tender. Serves 4 to 6.

SOUTHERN-STYLE SQUIRREL STEW

4 to 5 squirrels, cut in serving pieces
8 small white onions
1 bay leaf
1 1/2 cups diced celery
4 teaspoons salt
1/8 teaspoon pepper
2 quarts boiling water
2 cups diced, pared carrots
2 1/2 cups diced, pared potatoes
1/2 pound sliced, fresh mushrooms
1 can corn
1/2 cup flour
1/4 cup cold water
1 teaspoon snipped parsley
dash of tabasco sauce

Wash and dry cleaned squirrels. Place in kettle with onions, bay leaf, celery, salt, pepper, water. Simmer, covered, 2 hours or until squirrels are nearly tender. Add carrots, potatoes, mushrooms, corn. Simmer, covered, 30 minutes or until all is tender. Blend flour with water. Stir into stew. Cook until thickened. Add parsley, tabasco. Serves 6, or makes enough to feed 4 hungry hunters.

FRUITED SQUIRREL

2 squirrels, cut in serving pieces
12 prunes
1/4 cup raisins
3 tablespoons vinegar
6 gingersnaps, crumbled
1/2 teaspoon salt
pinch of mixed whole pickling spices
1 medium onion, fine-diced
3 tablespoons brown sugar
1 tablespoon butter
2 tablespoons flour, browned

Cook squirrel in salted water to cover until tender. Remove meat. To liquid add all ingredients except flour, simmer a few minutes. Thicken with flour dissolved in 1/4 cup cold water. Add meat, heat thoroughly. Serves 4.

SQUIRREL POT PIE

Cut squirrels in serving pieces, dredge in flour and brown in fat or salad oil. Place in kettle with tight lid. Add 1 quart boiling water, 1/4 lemon, sliced very thin, 1 teaspoon salt, 1/4 cup sherry, 1 onion, minced, and sautéed until brown in 1 tablespoon butter. Cover pan tightly and simmer 1 hour, or until meat is tender. Make a recipe of short biscuit dough, cut in rounds and place gently on top of squirrel. Cover pot tightly and simmer 15 minutes. Pile squirrel on platter and arrange dumplings around it. Thicken gravy with 1 tablespoon flour browned in 1 tablespoon butter. Pour gravy over meat and dumplings.

BRUNSWICK STEW

2 squirrels
1 tablespoon salt
1 onion, minced
2 cups lima beans
6 ears corn
1/2 pound salt pork
6 potatoes
1 teaspoon pepper
2 teaspoons sugar
4 cups sliced tomatoes
1/4 pound butter
flour
2 slices lemon

Cut squirrels in pieces as for fricassee. Add the salt to 4 quarts water and bring to boil; add onion, beans, corn, pork, potatoes, pepper and squirrel pieces. Cover tightly and simmer 2 hours. Add sugar and tomatoes, and simmer 1 hour more. Ten minutes before removing stew from stove, add butter cut into walnut-size pieces and rolled in flour. Boil up, adding salt or pepper if needed. Pour into tureen and garnish with lemon. Serves 4.

SQUIRREL AND DUMPLINGS

Cut 2 squirrels in serving pieces. Place in a kettle, cover with 1 inch water, add 2 bay leaves and simmer

1 1/4 hours, skimming as necessary. Add 1 cup sliced onions, 1 cup chopped celery, 10 medium carrots, quartered. Season with 2 teaspoons salt and 1/2 teaspoon pepper; add 1 1/2 cups hot water. Cook 15 minutes longer. Add dumplings (below). Serves 4.

Dumplings

2 cups flour
1/2 teaspoon salt
4 teaspoons baking powder
3/4 cup milk

Mix dry ingredients. Gradually add milk. Turn dough onto floured board, roll to 1/2-inch thickness, and cut in 3-inch squares. Place on top of ingredients in kettle, cover tightly, cook 15 minutes.

BAKED SQUIRREL

4 squirrels
flour
1 can bouillon
1/4 cup worcestershire sauce
2 tablespoons chopped parsley
2 tablespoons onion juice
1 clove garlic
1 small bay leaf
salt, pepper

Dredge squirrels with flour, brown in roasting pan. Add remaining ingredients. Bake in 350°F. oven 45 minutes. Reduce heat; bake slowly until tender. Serves 4 to 6.

SQUIRREL JAMBALAYA

1 medium squirrel
salt, red pepper
3 tablespoons cooking oil
2 large onions, chopped
3 stalks celery, chopped
1 clove garlic, chopped (optional)
1/4 green pepper, chopped
4 tablespoons chopped parsley
2 cups uncooked rice, washed
1 1/2 cups water
2 teaspoons salt

Cut squirrel into serving pieces; season well with salt and red pepper. Sauté squirrel in oil until brown; remove from skillet. Sauté onions, celery, garlic, green pepper and parsley in oil until wilted. Put squirrel back into skillet; cover. Cook slowly about 30 minutes or until squirrel is tender. Add rice and water. Stir thoroughly 2 to 3 minutes. Add salt; cook slowly about 30 minutes or until rice is cooked. Serves 2 to 4.

SQUIRREL IN CREAM SAUCE

4 to 6 squirrels
salt, pepper
flour
1/2 cup milk
1/2 cup cream
1/2 cup chopped celery
1/2 cup chopped onions
small can mushrooms

Cut meat into small pieces, salt and pepper lightly, and roll in flour. Brown pieces of floured meat in skillet, and then put them into covered dish for baking. Cover pieces with milk and cream and add chopped onions and chopped celery along with mushrooms. Bake in 350°F. oven until done, about 1 hour or longer. Serves 6 to 8.

SQUIRREL WITH GAME SAUCE

Place 4 squirrels on a rack in roaster and bake, covered, in 350°F. oven 1 hour, basting every 15 minutes with butter. Increase heat to 425°F. and bake 15 minutes longer with cover off roaster. Serve with Game Sauce (below). Serves 6.

Game Sauce

1/2 cup grape jelly
1/2 cup currant jelly
1/4 cup butter
1 tablespoon orange juice concentrate mixed with 2 tablespoons water
2 tablespoons grated lemon rind
2 tablespoons grated orange rind
1/2 cup sherry

Melt jellies in saucepan with the butter. Add orange juice and rinds. Bring to a boil, remove from fire. Add sherry.

SQUIRREL FAIRFIELD STEW

2 squirrels
3 quarts water
1 large onion, minced
2 cups dried lima beans, soaked
1 can cream style corn
1/2 pound butter
1 tablespoon salt
1/2 teaspoon pepper
1 large potato, quartered
1 No. 2-can tomatoes, sliced
4 tablespoons sugar

Disjoint squirrels and place in deep kettle with water, onion, lima beans, corn, 1/4 pound butter, 1 tablespoon salt, 1/2 teaspoon pepper, and any other of your favorite seasonings. Cover and simmer 2 hours. Add potatoes, tomatoes, and sugar. Simmer 1 hour longer. About 15 minutes before stew is finished, add another 1/4 pound butter. Serves 4.

SQUIRREL SUPREME

2 squirrels
1 medium apple
3 tablespoons butter OR shortening
salt, pepper
1 large onion, sliced
1 1/2 cups diced carrots
1/2 cup diced rutabaga
1 1/2 cups water

Cut squirrels into serving pieces. Clean and wash thoroughly. Put into large kettle, cover with water; add cut-up apple including seeds and core. Bring to boil and cook about 15 minutes. (Watch carefully, as it boils over easily.) Remove meat from kettle and rinse in warm water. Drain. Melt butter or shortening in frying pan, add meat and brown. Salt and pepper to taste. When meat is browned add onion, carrots, rutabaga and water. Cover and let cook on low heat until meat and vegetables are tender and water has evaporated. More water may be added if it becomes too dry during cooking time—2 to 3 hours. Serves 4.

SQUIRREL WITH WHITE WINE

4 squirrels, cut in serving pieces
2 tablespoons butter
1/4 cup olive oil
salt, pepper
2 cloves garlic, crushed
1/2 teaspoon rosemary
1 cup dry white wine
1 cup chicken broth
1 tablespoon chopped parsley
2 cups sliced mushrooms

Sauté squirrel in butter and oil until lightly browned; add salt and pepper to taste, garlic, rosemary, wine and broth; simmer until nearly done, turning often. Add parsley and mushrooms, cook 5 minutes. Serves 4.

CREAMED SQUIRREL ON RICE

3 squirrels, cooked
1 can cream of mushroom soup
1 soup-can of milk
onion salt
steamed rice

Bone all pieces of squirrel and cut meat into large pieces. Dilute mushroom soup with can of milk and heat. Add meat to warmed soup, season with onion salt to taste. Serve over steamed rice. Serves 4 to 6.

SQUIRREL HUNTER'S STEW

2 squirrels
1 cup vinegar
1 onion, diced
3/4 teaspoon salt
1/4 teaspoon pepper
1 1/4 teaspoons mixed spices
leaves from 3 stalks celery
2 carrots, diced

Wash dressed squirrel thoroughly and cut into serving pieces. Combine next 4 ingredients in deep container. Add squirrel and enough water to cover. Let stand 3 hours. Drain squirrel, brown in 375°F. oven. Add remaining ingredients and again cover with water. Cover pan and continue cooking until tender. Serves 2 to 3.

SOUTHERN FRIED SQUIRREL

Skin and disjoint 2 squirrels. Drop pieces slowly into boiling water to cover. Cut up and add:

1 onion
1 carrot
1 stalk celery
1 sprig parsley

Simmer until tender. Cool thoroughly. Dry squirrel pieces between towels. Prepare batter (below). Dip each piece of squirrel into batter, then drop into deep hot fat and fry until pieces are golden brown. Serve with gravy made of stock and cream. Serves 4.

Batter

1/2 cup flour
1/2 cup cornmeal
1 teaspoon baking powder
1/4 teaspoon salt
1 beaten egg
3/4 cup milk

Mix dry ingredients. Beat egg lightly. Add milk. Stir liquid into dry ingredients.

SQUIRREL CHOWDER

2 squirrels
chicken parts, as desired
1 pound lean beef, cubed
1 cup celery, sliced
1 can corn
2 medium onions, sliced
salt, pepper
1 can tomato juice
1 can green beans
4 potatoes, cubed
3 carrots, sliced
1 can peas

Combine meat, celery, corn, onions, salt and pepper. Cover with water. Cook until meat is almost tender. Add tomato juice, green beans, potatoes, carrots and peas. Cook until tender. Remove bones and serve. Serves 4 to 6.

SQUIRREL CAKES

3 squirrels
2 tablespoons breadcrumbs
1 onion, fine-chopped
1 tablespoon catsup
1/2 cup mashed potatoes

Parboil squirrels in salt water for about 15 minutes, then remove all good meat. Grind bits of meat and blend with the breadcrumbs, onion, catsup, and mashed potatoes. Mix well. Shape into small flat cakes and sauté in hot bacon fat until well browned. Serves 4.

BIG GAME

When you approach the big-game animal that your bullet has just dropped, the main object of your hunt has been attained. Before you are enough steaks, chops, roasts, stew meat, and other cuts to provide the normal American family with its meat requirements for many hearty meals. Getting the meat out of the woods in perfect shape and into a freezing locker or refrigerator is now your only problem, and it's important your solution to that problem allows none of the meat to go to waste.

Accurate shooting, of course, provides the best meat. When a wounded animal runs off to die at a distance from the hunter, its exertions will have sent the blood coursing through its body, into its muscles, affecting both tenderness and flavor. And if the hunter fails to reach the animal until some time after it has died, all or almost all of the blood may remain in the body, further toughening the meat and making it much more likely to spoil.

Approach your game carefully from behind, since the greatest danger lies in being struck by the sharp hoofs of a wounded animal. If the animal is still alive, a shot through the neck just under the ear will kill it cleanly and will help bleed it as well, for such a shot will sever the jugular vein.

DEER

The deer should be bled at once. Failure to do this immediately will impair the quality of the meat. Insert a sharp knife at the base of the neck, where it joins the chest (brisket), and cut the artery at that point. Keep the wound open and free of clotting blood. The more blood drained off the better.

If the deer can be dressed out immediately, "sticking" or bleeding, although it is still advisable, is not quite so necessary. To accomplish the dressing out with some ease hang the deer by its head or place it on sloping ground with its head and back on the upslope. A piece of stout rope, or a long length of heavy line that can be doubled for strength, should be carried by every deer hunter to use for such purposes. You can pull the deer up over a limb with it, work it up on a tripod, or at least lift the head and forward part of the body off the ground. If the deer is dressed out while lying on the ground, a piece of rope comes in handy to tie one hind leg to a bush or a rock to keep it out of your way while you work.

Use a very sharp and sturdy knife, one with a thin blade. A large pocket knife will do well enough if it sets rigidly and its blade is well honed. The smaller sheath knives are, of course, better than the large ones. If you have any doubt about the type of knife to use, ask your butcher's advice.

Take your time. You'll find satisfaction in doing a good job. The operation is simple enough and need not be a messy one, unless the deer is badly shot up—another good argument for accurate shooting. It will save you trouble and waste less meat.

Make a cut through the hide and belly muscle, beginning at the point where the breastbone ends and moving downward to a point just short of the tail. Be careful not to puncture any of the organs while making the cut. Cut around the genitals on both sides and cut the hide in a complete circle around the anus. Next, pull out the large intestine. The genitals and anus will come out with it. If you have an ax handy you can split the pelvic bones to simplify removal of the intestines and to permit the carcass to cool more rapidly. Remove the heart, lungs, and other organs. The windpipe can be severed at the sticking point. Using a dry cloth or moss and leaves, clean any remaining free blood out of the inside of the deer. Don't use water. Some hunters carry a piece of clean burlap or a roll of paper towels.

As soon as they are cleaned and cooled, the heart and liver are ready for cooking and are usually a welcome bit of camp meat. The torn and bloodshot meat around the wound should be separated from the rest of the carcass and saved. It can be soaked for about 10 hours in cold, salted water and then used as ground meat.

Carelessness, delay in dressing out, or failure to cool the deer meat completely and quickly are things to avoid. The carcass should hang in a cool place with one or two sticks cut to the right length inserted between the walls of the body cavity to permit free circulation of air. Deer hide is an excellent insulating layer, and unless cool air can flow freely to the open flesh, the cooling may take many hours.

Now that your deer is dressed you've got to get him to the highway or camp. The easiest way is to drag him, especially if you're hunting on snow-covered terrain. A short rope, even a belt, fitted with a crossbar handle will serve this purpose. The deer will drag easily when pulled from the lower jaw. So, cut the skin and flesh just behind the bone at the point of the jaw and pass the line or belt through the slit.

Whenever the deer reaches its final destination, the carcass should be hung immediately (either by the hind legs or head) and the sides propped open while the cooling process is continued.

Much meat spoilage occurs while the carcass is traveling from

hunting area to camp site or home. No one would walk into a meat market and buy a roast, then strap it to a fender and drive a hundred miles or more, subjecting it to all kinds of dirt, and still eat it.

Why not go hunting prepared to handle your game properly? Along with your knife, carry a saw, hatchet or ax, and a quantity of clean cheesecloth. The latter is necessary to wrap meat in once you've skinned and quartered your deer. Covering the meat with cheesecloth or fine netting not only protects meat from dust and grime, but from insects if the weather is warm enough to provide them. Once wrapped, pack the meat securely in your car in a place where fresh air can reach it freely, rather than subjecting it to dust from the open road. In warm weather, however, don't put your deer quartered or otherwise, in the trunk of your car with the lid closed. Leave the lid ajar to permit air to circulate. As a word of caution, check state laws regarding requirements that evidence of sex must not be destroyed or that carcasses must be kept whole.

Before butchering, the deer should be skinned. The hide can be used to make articles of clothing for the outdoors. If you plan to use the hide, cover the flesh side with a thorough coating of salt. After a day, remove the first coating and renew the salt layer. Then fold the hide with the flesh side in and ship immediately to a taxidermist or tan it yourself.

To prepare a head for mounting, the "cape" or neck-and-head skin should be cut, and the skin removed from the neck to the head. The skin is withdrawn from around the base of the horns. Then the ear cartilage is severed just under the skin, and the skin of the lips and nostrils is worked free. Use great care not to cut it with the knife yet, leaving a minimum of flesh. Care should also be taken not to trim too closely at the lips and eyes. Salt should be rubbed thoroughly into the flesh side of the skin and into the ears, nostrils, eyelids, and mouth. It is important not to overlook any part of the flesh side of the skin when making this salt covering since the hair may drop out of the other side from failure to salt completely. The cape should be folded with the salted side in, kept in a cool place, and shipped to a taxidermist together with the skull from which all flesh has been removed. A good photograph of the head before skinning will aid the taxidermist in making a true-to-life mount. If shipment to the taxidermist is delayed, check the salt covering on the flesh side of the cape skin and resalt any thinly covered sections.

Refrigerator storage is the most satisfactory way of preserving venison for the average hunter, and it's usually preferable to have the butcher who is going to store your deer prepare the meat as well. However, if you have a place to work and the simple tools required, it isn't too difficult to do the job yourself.

QUARTER HERE

Hang the carcass by the hocks and saw it in half down the backbone. An ordinary handsaw will do. Then take each half and cut according to the accompanying diagram. The loin will give the best roasts or steaks (sirloin or porterhouse). The chuck and rump are good for pot roasts and ground meat. The round will make good steaks unless the animal is particularly tough, and then it may be ground up or used as swiss steaks. If the leg is small it may be roasted all in one piece in the manner of a leg of lamb. The shank, neck, flank, and spareribs can best be used for soups and stews—cut in cubes—or ground up. With tendons removed the neck should be tender—it will make a good roast.

Much of the foregoing can also be applied to the handling of elk, caribou, moose, and antelope.

Some people complain about the strong flavor and/or odor of the venison either before or after preparing it for eating. These two conditions can be controlled by the person who kills the deer and brings it home. Strong flavor and odor result from improper bleeding of the animal at time of kill, improper dressing of the animal, improper cooling out, and bloody tissues and membranes.

To prevent these problems, get to the animal as soon as possible after it is down and cut the blood vessel in the neck. Open the abdominal cavity immediately and remove all internal organs as well as genital organs and anus. Wipe the internal cavity clean of all blood—it is a good idea to carry a large piece of muslin for this purpose. In cutting open the animal be very careful not to puncture or cut the stomach or intestines. Material from the stomach or intestines will taint any meat it comes in contact with and develop an unpleasant flavor.

As soon as the animal is completely cleaned out inside, hang it by the head in the shade. If no tree is available from which to hang it, gather brush and pile it sufficiently high to hold the animal at least six inches off the ground. Lay the animal across the brush with the stomach opening up. Cut sticks an inch or so thick and of a length that will hold the abdominal walls of the animal as wide open as possible. All of this is necessary to reduce the body heat quickly. An animal can develop a strong odor and flavor in its meat if left lying on the ground, even though it is dressed out, because the skin and hair of the animal are like a fur coat—they hold the body heat in the flesh much longer than if the animal is suspended so that air can circulate around and through it.

Venison is a rather dry meat, usually improved by adding suet or butter in cooking. The characteristic flavor is largely in the fat, so removal of most fat will make the taste less "gamey."

WILD GAME RAGOUT

3 pounds venison, elk, caribou,
moose, or antelope
3 tablespoons olive oil
3 large onions, chopped
5 garlic cloves, crushed
1/2 pound bacon, chopped
1 teaspoon curry powder
1 can tomato soup, undiluted
1 1/2 quarts water
2 teaspoons bourbon
1/4 cup beer
1 tablespoon salt
1/2 pound fresh mushrooms, sliced

Cut meat into cubes about 1 1/2 inches square. Heat olive oil in electric skillet and add meat, onions, garlic and bacon. Cook until all is richly browned, stirring frequently. Add all other ingredients except mushrooms; cover and simmer for 50 minutes. Add mushrooms and simmer 10 minutes more. Serve over rice. Serves 8.

You do not need to marinate game before using; in fact, it is better if you do not. This dish reheats well and can be prepared a day ahead.

ONION-ROASTED VENISON

4 pound rump OR shoulder roast
cooking fat
salt, pepper
1 package dry onion-soup mix
1/2 cup water

Brown roast in cooking fat on all sides on top of stove. Season with salt and pepper. Sprinkle package of onion soup mix on and around roast. Add water. Cook in 300°F. oven, in covered pan, until tender. Serves 6.

BUTTERMILK-BASTED VENISON

Wash roast under running water, cut off all fat, and brown vension, seasoned with salt, garlic powder, and pepper. Put in roaster, stick toothpicks in meat, and drop raw onion rings over toothpicks. Pour 1 quart buttermilk over roast and bake in 375°F. oven to degree of cooking desired. Save liquid from roast and use to heat any leftover meat another day.

VENISON MINCEMEAT

3 pounds venison,
cooked and ground
1 lemon, ground
3 pounds seedless raisins
1 pound seeded raisins
1/2 pound currants
1 pound ground suet
6 pounds pared chopped apples
1 pint grape juice
1 quart cider OR apple juice
2 teaspoons cinnamon
1 teaspoon ground cloves
1 teaspoon allspice
1 teaspoon salt
3 cups sugar

117

Combine all ingredients. Cook in large pan on low heat 3 hours, or until apples are tender. Cool. Store in refrigerator or freezer. Makes 8 quarts.

BURGUNDY-ROASTED VENISON

6- to 7-pound leg of venison
(if lower part of leg is used,
remove shank bone)
2 cups burgundy
1 cup beef bouillon
1 medium onion, sliced
1 clove garlic, crushed
1 bay leaf
3 juniper berries (optional)
1 teaspoon salt
6 slices salt pork

Place meat in large bowl. Cover with marinade made from the wine, bouillon, onion, garlic, bay leaf, juniper berries, and salt. Put in refrigerator for 24 hours. Remove meat; either tie or skewer in compact shape. Strain marinade and reserve. Place meat on rack in shallow pan. Arrange slices of salt pork over top. Roast, uncovered, in 450°F. oven 10 minutes. Reduce heat to 325°F. and roast 15 to 18 minutes per pound, to an internal temperature of 140°F. for very rare, 150°F. for medium well done. Baste meat occasionally with reserved marinade. Strain drippings, discard fat, and serve drippings over sliced roast. Serves 8 to 10.

POT ROAST OF VENISON

haunch or loin of venison
salt pork
3 medium-size onions
4 carrots
2 small turnips
4 stalks of celery
parsley
pinch of rosemary
pinch of thyme
2 bay leaves
2 strips lemon peel
salt
8 peppercorns
dry red wine
sour cream

Trim carefully and remove all surplus fibers, skin, and fat from venison haunch or loin. Prepare and lard with salt pork. Place the sliced vegetables and fine-chopped herbs in a dutch oven with equal parts red wine and water, bring to a boil, and let simmer for 30 minutes. Add the larded venison and cover. Simmer for 2 hours. Remove meat, strain the sauce, and place venison in a roasting pan. Pour the strained liquid over the roast, adding 1/2 cup of sour cream, and cook slowly until well done.

PORT-MARINATED VENISON STEAKS

Put venison steaks to half the depth of a 2-gallon stone crock and distribute 1 pound brown sugar between steaks. Fill crock with port wine. Let stand 24 hours. Remove steaks and broil or cook in whatever manner you like. Steaks should not remain in marinade more than 24 hours. Marinade can be reused for other steaks.

Don't confine yourself to venison— this works wonders with almost any type big-game steak.

SWEET-SOUR VENISON

venison steaks OR roast
6 tablespoons olive oil
1 1/2 teaspoons salt
1 1/2 cups brown sugar
2 teaspoons mustard
2 tablespoons vinegar

Brown meat in oil, place in dutch oven or covered roaster. Combine remaining ingredients to make sauce. Layer steak with sauce. If roasting meat use sauce to cover roast and to baste frequently while cooking. Bake in 400°F. oven 20 minutes per pound.

CHICKEN-FRIED VENISON ROUND STEAK

Cut round steaks 3/4 inch thick into serving-size pieces. If necessary, carefully cut out tough membranes. Pound each piece with steak tenderizer or back of a heavy butcher knife. Season with garlic or onion salt and fresh-ground black pepper. Dredge in seasoned flour. Fry in a heavy skillet in 1/4 inch of fairly hot shortening, browning well on both sides. Drain steaks on paper toweling and keep warm. Pour off all but 3 tablespoons fat. Add 3 tablespoons flour; heat, stirring, until bubbly. Add 1 1/2 cups milk; cook, stirring, until thickened. Taste and correct seasoning if necessary.

VENISON STROGANOFF

1 pound venison steak cut in
long, thin strips
3 tablespoons flour
salt, pepper
1 onion
1 cup tomato juice
1 1/2 cups water
1 teaspoon sugar
1 can mushrooms
1/2 cup sour cream

Dredge meat with flour and salt and pepper. Brown lightly in fat with the onion. Add tomato juice, water, sugar. Simmer until tender. Ten minutes before serving, add mushrooms, sour cream. Serves 4.

GINGER VENISON ROAST

1 3 1/2-to 4-pound venison roast
1 bay leaf
1 medium onion, diced
3 whole allspice
salt, pepper
1 package gingersnap cookies

Place meat in roasting pan and season with bay leaf, onion, allspice, pepper and salt. Lay gingersnaps on top and sides of roast. Place in a 325°F. oven about 3 hours, or until tender. Remove gingersnaps, prepare gravy. Serves 6.

SAUSAGE-STUFFED VENISON

Remove bone from 8- to 10-pound hind quarter of venison. Place a long Polish sausage in the cavity. Season roast with salt and pepper and garlic (optional). Place 6 strips of bacon over roast. Tear off 2 strips heavy-duty aluminum foil and fasten together with a double fold. Place roast in center and add 2 cups burgundy. Close foil and place on baking sheet. Bake in 350°F. oven 4 to 6 hours, depending on degree of cooking desired. Open foil and bake another 30 minutes to brown roast. Make gravy with the drippings in the foil. Serves 8 to 10.

PAN-FRIED VENISON STEAKS

1 pound "ham" steaks,
1/2-inch thick
1/4 cup thick cream OR
evaporated milk
1/4 cup flour
3 tablespoons butter OR margarine
salt, pepper, garlic salt

Pound steaks thoroughly with sharp-edged meat pounder. Cut into serving pieces. Dip steaks into cream or milk, dredge in flour, and brown one side in hot butter or margarine. Turn. Season with salt and pepper and garlic salt to taste. Continue cooking until second side is well browned. Serve hot. Serves 4.

TASTY VENISON HEART

1 venison heart
1 cup red wine
2 tablespoons vinegar
1 teaspoon salt
2 peppercorns
1 teaspoon prepared mustard
1 medium-size onion, sliced
1 bay leaf
flour
2 tablespoons butter

Split heart in half (top to bottom), remove all vents and ducts, and soak halves in a marinade of wine, vinegar, salt, peppercorns, mustard, onion, and bay leaf. After marinating, roll hearts in flour and place in butter in a hot skillet. Sear thoroughly. Reduce heat slightly and cook about 5 minutes. Serves 4.

BRAISED VENISON CHOPS

Roll chops in flour well-seasoned with salt and pepper. Brown well in shortening. Add 1/2 cup water and simmer until tender. Pour 1 cup of burgundy or claret wine over chops and cook down until almost dry. Remove chops and make gravy, adding 1 small can of mushrooms. Simmer 3 minutes. Pour gravy over chops before serving.

VENISON MEAT LOAF

1/2 pound salt pork
2 pounds ground venison
1/2 cup chopped onion
1/4 cup chopped celery
1/4 cup chopped parsley
1 cup soft bread crumbs
1 cup milk or canned or
cooked tomatoes
1 egg, beaten
1 teaspoon salt

Cut salt pork in small pieces and fry until lightly browned. Mix with remaining ingredients. Mold mixture into a loaf. Place on foil in uncovered pan on rack. Bake in a 350°F. oven 1 1/4 to 2 hours. Serves 8 to 10.

MARINATED VENISON

1/2 cup salad oil
1 cup dry red wine
6 sprigs parsley
2 cloves garlic, crushed
1 bay leaf
1/2 teaspoon dried thyme
1 medium onion cut in half
stuck with 2 cloves
6 peppercorns
3 pounds sliced venison,
shoulder, breast or flank
Butter or oil
2 tablespoons flour

Combine all ingredients except venison, oil, flour; marinate the meat in this mixture overnight. Drain and pat dry. Sauté the meat in a little butter or oil until brown. Arrange in a baking dish. Strain the marinade and heat to boiling. Thicken with the flour mixed with 1/4 cup water. Pour over venison, and bake in a 350°F. oven for 40 to 45 minutes. Serve with crusty bread, parslied rice and cucumber salad. Serves 6 to 8.

DEER STEW

Brown 2 to 3 pounds deer meat, cut into pieces, in bacon fat. Add 2 large sliced onions and continue browning. When nicely browned stir in 3 tablespoons flour. Place in baking dish and add: 2 tablespoons vinegar, 3 tablespoons catsup, 1 tablespoon sugar, and salt and pepper to taste. Cover meat with water and bake in 375°F. oven for 2 to 3 hours, or until tender, adding water as needed to keep meat covered. When done, thicken gravy and serve. Serves 4 to 6.

VENISON POTATO SAUSAGE

4 pounds venison
1 pound beef
2 pounds lean pork
1 large onion
1/2 peck potatoes
2 tablespoons salt
1 teaspoon pepper
1 teaspoon allspice
1 pound casings

Grind all the meat and the onion. Then wash, peel, and grind the potatoes. Mix together and add salt and pepper and allspice. Mix thoroughly. Use a sausage stuffer and do not stuff the casings too full. After stuffing, tie the ends of the sausages with string. Submerge in large kettle of cold water and bring to a boil. Boil about 1 hour at 325°F. Prick each sausage with a fork after the first 10 minutes of boiling. Sausages can be served hot or cold, or may be stored in a cold place for use at a later time. Sausage flavor is at its best when fried in skillet until casings are golden brown.

VENISON-STUFFED CABBAGE LEAVES

2 pounds ground venison
5 tablespoons chopped onion
3 tablespoons butter
2 cups cooked rice
1 tablespoon chopped dill OR
1/2 teaspoon dill salt
pepper to taste
salt
12 cabbage leaves
1 8-ounce can tomato sauce

Brown venison and onion in butter. Mix in rice, chopped dill or dill salt, and pepper to taste. (If dill salt is used, use regular salt sparingly, if necessary. If dill or dill salt is not handy, simply use regular salt.) Place 12 large cabbage leaves in boiling water for 1 minute. Drain and dry on paper toweling. Place the meat mixture in the center of each leaf, fold leaf over, and secure with toothpicks. Place filled leaves in greased baking dish. Pour tomato sauce over leaves and bake in 325°F. oven about 45 minutes. Serves 6.

BROILED VENISON STEAKS OR CHOPS

Preheat the broiling oven, and place steaks or chops on greased rack in broiler about 3 inches from flame. Leave oven door open slightly. Broil on one side until nicely brown (5 to 7 minutes), then turn to other side for a similar period. Venison should be cooked rare but well-browned on the surface. Serve at once, seasoned with salt and pepper or Parsley Butter (below).

Parsley Butter

1/2 cup butter or margarine
1/2 teaspoon salt
dash of pepper
1/4 teaspoon chopped parsley
3/4 tablespoon lemon juice

Work butter or margarine until creamy. Then add salt, pepper, parsley, and finally the lemon juice, very slowly.

VENISON SAUERBRATEN

4 pounds venison pot roast,
3 to 4 inches thick
2 cups vinegar
2 cups water
2 cups onions, sliced
4 bay leaves
16 whole cloves
1 tablespoon salt
1/4 teaspoon pepper
2 tablespoons sugar
5 tablespoons fat
12 gingersnaps

Cover meat with vinegar and water, onions, bay leaves, cloves, salt and pepper, and sugar. Let stand in refrigerator for 24 hours. Remove from marinade and wipe dry. Brown meat in hot fat. Place meat on rack in heavy 4-quart skillet or dutch oven. Strain marinade and add 3 cups to pan. Cover. Simmer slowly about 2 1/2 hours or roast in 350°F. oven about 2 1/2 hours. Thicken gravy with crumbled gingersnaps. Serves 6 to 8.

MISSOURI VENISON STEW

3 to 4 pounds venison
flour
3 tablespoons bacon fat
1 1/2 cups hot water
1 cup red wine
1 teaspoon mixed dry thyme,
marjoram, basil
1 teaspoon dried parsley
1 large onion, sliced
1 1/2 teaspoons salt
1/2 teaspoon coarse pepper
3 carrots, scraped and quartered
3 potatoes, peeled and quartered

Remove sinews and bones from venison, cut meat into bite-size pieces, and roll in flour. Brown in hot bacon fat in deep kettle. Add hot water, wine, herbs, onions, and salt and pepper. Cover pot and bring to a boil. Lower heat and simmer 2 hours. Add carrots and potatoes. Cover and simmer 1 hour, adding more hot water if needed. When meat is tender and vegetables done, serve hot. Serves 6.

BARBECUED SHORT RIBS OF VENISON

Have ribs cut in 3-inch lengths, with 2 or 3 ribs for each serving. Place pieces of rib in a roasting pan; cover with water. Add 1 medium onion, sliced, 1 tablespoon diced garlic, 1 tablespoon seasoned salt, 1/4 teaspoon pepper. Cover and simmer over low heat for 1 hour. Drain, reserving liquid. Pour over ribs a homemade or bottled barbecue sauce to cover. Add 1 cup of reserved liquid. Bake, uncovered, in 350°F. oven, adding more barbecue sauce and/or liquid as necessary, until meat is fork tender.

This is a tasty way to prepare a portion of the animal generally discarded. The recipe works equally well for short ribs of elk or of antelope.

PAN-BROILED VENISON CHOPS

Cut chops 1/2 inch thick. Heat a heavy cast-iron skillet until it is smoking. Wrap a piece of bacon around the tines of a fork and wipe it quickly over the bottom of the skillet. Put the chops in the skillet and sear well, about 2 to 3 minutes on each side. Serve immediately on hot plate and season to taste.

JOHNSON DEER LOAF

1 pound ground venison
1/2 pound ground lean pork
12 salted crackers, crushed
1/4 cup catsup and 1/4 cup
chili sauce OR 1/2 cup catsup
1 egg
1 small onion, grated
salt, pepper
1 tablespoon minced green pepper
1/8 teaspoon prepared mustard
1/8 teaspoon celery seed
1/8 teaspoon garlic salt
2 teaspoons worcestershire sauce
1/8 teaspoon crushed savory leaf
dash of curry powder
parmesan cheese
2 or 3 beef OR chicken
bouillon cubes

Grease loaf pan. Combine ingredients, except cheese, bouillon cubes, pour 1 cup of water over, and mix well. Form into loaf. Sprinkle with cheese. Bake in 350°F. oven 1 3/4 hours. When making gravy, use drippings, and add 2 or 3 beef or chicken bouillon cubes. Serves 6.

HAWAIIAN VENISON

1 pound venison steaks
1/4 cup flour
1/4 cup butter
1/2 cup boiling water
1 teaspoon salt
2 to 3 green peppers
1/2 cup pineapple chunks

Cut steaks into 1-inch cubes, cover with flour, and brown in hot fat. Add water and salt and simmer until tender. Clean peppers, cut into 1-inch squares, and boil 10 minutes. Then drain. Add pineapple chunks and pepper squares to browned meat. Pour Hawaiian Sauce (below) over meat mixture and simmer 5 minutes. Serve over Chinese noodles or cooked rice. Serves 4 to 6.

Hawaiian Sauce

2 1/2 teaspoons cornstarch
1/2 cup pineapple juice
1/4 cup vinegar
1/2 cup sugar
2 1/2 teaspoons soy sauce

Combine ingredients and cook until sauce thickens.

VENISON SHORT RIBS

3 pounds venison short ribs
1 tablespoon salt
1 quart water
1 teaspoon paprika
1 large onion, chopped
1/2 cup catsup
1/4 cup vinegar
2 tablespoons water
2 teaspoons chili powder
3 tablespoons bacon drippings

Soak venison ribs in salt-water solution for several hours or overnight. Wash the ribs after soaking and parboil about 30 minutes in pressure cooker at 10 pounds pressure. Remove from pressure cooker and place in frying pan. Mix the last 7 ingredients together, pour over ribs, and bake in 375°F. oven about 1 hour, or until meat is tender and browned. Serves 4 to 6.

BOHEMIAN PICKLED VENISON WITH CREAM GRAVY

venison roast
salt
1 1/2 cups vinegar
3 cups water
1 large onion, sliced
6 whole cloves
10 whole allspice
10 black peppercorns
1 bay leaf
lemon rind
1 1/3 cups sour cream
1 teaspoon flour
1 egg yolk, beaten

Trim venison roast and dust with salt. Combine vinegar, 2 cups water, onion, and spices, cover, and boil together 15 minutes. Then let cool and pour over venison roast. Let marinate 2 to 3 days, turning once or twice each day. When ready to bake, place in baking pan, add about 1/2 of the marinade, remaining cup of water, and a piece of lemon rind. Bake in 325°F oven 25 to 30 minutes per pound. When about half done, baste with 1/3 cup sour cream. Turn over once while baking and baste frequently. When done, remove roast. Add remaining cup sour cream to the liquid. Thicken with flour and beaten egg yolk. Strain sauce and serve with potatoes or dumplings.

HUNTER'S VENISON PIE

1 1/2 to 2 pounds venison roast
1 tablespoon butter
3 diced onions
1 clove garlic, minced
1 can tomatoes
1 tablespoon paprika
pinch cayenne (optional)
1 bay leaf
dash of thyme
1 cup beer
2 to 3 carrots, sliced
1 cup frozen OR canned peas

Cut meat in 1-inch squares, removing fat and sinew. Heat butter in skillet and brown meat quickly to retain juices. Add onions, garlic, tomatoes, and other seasonings, then the beer. Cover and cook slowly until meat is tender, about 1 to 2 hours. Add carrots and peas when meat is almost tender. (If dish is to be served as a stew, without a Biscuit Topping [below], 4 potatoes which have been peeled and quartered, may be added with the carrots and peas.) Remove from heat and pour into baking dish. Drop Biscuit Topping batter from spoon and bake in 425°F.

oven 25 minutes, or until topping is nicely browned. Serves 4.

Biscuit Topping

1 cup flour
3/4 cup yellow cornmeal
1 tablespoon sugar
1 tablespoon baking powder
1/2 teaspoon salt
3/4 cup milk
3 tablespoons melted shortening
1 egg, slightly beaten

Combine flour, cornmeal, sugar, baking powder, and salt in mixing bowl. Add milk, shortening, and egg, and stir until smooth.

MOOSE, CARIBOU, ELK

Methods employed for dressing and butchering moose, caribou, elk, and antelope are the same in general as those for deer, but animals larger than deer may present greater problems.

A piece of stout rope is likely to be extremely valuable in handling these larger animals, and a small ax or saw is essential to do a satisfactory job of dressing a moose or elk.

To split a backbone with an ax is no mean task and usually means the ax edge will have dulled considerably before the job is done and a healthy amount of wasted and mangled meat will be left in its wake. Splitting the carcass on either side of the backbone with an ax also results in poorer cuts than when the backbone is sawed in half. So a small saw is well worth the little extra cost.

A lightweight saw, one of the small, skeleton types, is best. The take-apart type hacksaw will also serve well if the teeth on the blade are larger than normal size. Which-ever your preference, choose a style that may be taken apart and folded compactly for transporting. You can reassemble it when needed.

All the cardinal rules for butchering meat must be kept in mind. Bleed quickly and thor-oughly. Dress out immediately. Cool completely and without delay. Protect from dirt, water, and insects.

If the animal must be packed on the backs of hunter and guide for any distance, pack sacks should be provided or improvised. It is impossible for one man to handle any of these animals, with the possible exception of the smaller antelope, in one piece. Big-game animals must be quartered to be carried, and if the hike is long and the loads heavy, a substantial amount of weight can be eliminated by cutting out the larger bones and discarding them.

The meat, of course, is all valuable, and these big animals carry a considerable amount of it on their ample frames.

Cultured buttermilk will tende-rize and remove much of the "gamey" or wild flavor and odor from the meat of deer, bear, moose, and elk. Cover meat completely with cultured buttermilk in a bowl. Steaks and chops should marinate 4 to 5 hours. Four-pound and heav-ier roasts should marinate 12 hours. After the meat has marinated, wipe off excess buttermilk with paper towels or a damp cloth. Cook the meat according to your favorite recipe—you will find it to be more tender and of delicious flavor.

STUFFED MOOSE STEAK

1 moose steak
1/2 teaspoon salt
1/8 teaspoon pepper
1/4 cup flour
3 cups breadcrumbs
3/4 cup onions, chopped
3/4 cup celery, chopped
1/2 cup butter
1/2 teaspoon paprika
1 sweet green pepper, sliced
dash of salt, pepper
sliced bacon

Season steak with salt and pepper, dip in flour, and pound well on both sides. Mix the next 7 ingredients to make stuffing and place on steak. Roll up and tie.

Set rolled steak in roasting pan. Place slices of bacon over steaks. Roast until tender in 325°F. oven, as it will improve the flavor.

MOOSE MEATLOAF

1 pound ground moose meat
2 eggs
2 tablespoons grated celery
2 tablespoons grated cheese
1/3 cup grated onion
1 teaspoon salt
1 teaspoon sage
dash black pepper
2/3 cup breadcrumbs
1 cup milk
catsup
1/2 cup water

Add ground moose meat, eggs, and other ingredients mixed together to breadcrumbs soaked in milk in a large mixing bowl. Mix well. Shape into a loaf and spread catsup on top. Place in greased pan. Add approximately 1/2 cup water around loaf. Cover and bake in 350°F. oven 1 hour. Serves 4.

MOOSE STEAK

1 moose steak
1/2 cup onions, chopped fine
2 tablespoons butter
1 cup chopped mushrooms
2 tablespoons flour
1/2 cup sweet (or sour) cream

Sauté onions in butter. Add steak and sear on both sides in butter and browned onion. Cover and let simmer for half an hour. When almost tender, add mushrooms and flour stirred into cream. Cover and let simmer for 20 minutes. Serves 4.

MOOSE CHILI

1/2 to 1 pound ground moose meat
1 tablespoon bacon fat
1 small onion, minced
1/2 to 1 green pepper, chopped
1 large can chili beans OR
kidney beans
1 medium-size can of tomatoes
salt, pepper
chili powder to taste

Brown meat in bacon fat, breaking the ground meat into small pieces as you brown it. Add onion and green pepper and cook until onion begins to brown, about 5 minutes. Stir often. Add beans, tomatoes, and salt and pepper, stirring occasionally, and enough chili powder to suit your taste. Cook about 1 hour over medium heat. Serves 4 to 6.

ROLLED MOOSE STEAK

Take a large, moose round steak, about 1/2-inch thick, and trim it into a square shape, about 12 inches to a side. Then, sauté 1/2 pound mushrooms with 1/2 a chopped onion in butter. Mix with 1 cup dry-toast crumbs, and 1 tablespoon worcestershire sauce. Sprinkle steak with pepper and garlic salt, spread with mushroom mixture, and roll up loosely, like a jelly roll. Tie in three places with string and sear on all sides in a dutch oven. Pour in 1 cup red wine and lower heat. Bake in 325°F. oven about 2 hours. Serves 8.

SWISS STYLE MOOSE STEAK

3 to 3 1/2 pounds of moose round
OR sirloin, cut into 1/2- or
3/4-inch slices
1 1/2 teaspoons meat tenderizer
1/2 cup flour
1/2 to 3/4 cup bacon fat
OR other shortening
1 to 2 cups water
1 1/2 to 2 teaspoons salt
1/4 teaspoon pepper
1 bay leaf
1/4 teaspoon sweet basil
1 onion
1 teaspoon worcestershire sauce

Sprinkle meat with tenderizer, dust meat with flour, then pound or rub it in. Brown meat in hot fat. When brown on each side, place in a 3 1/2-quart casserole. Add water and salt and pepper. Bake in 325°F. oven 2 hours. Then add remaining ingredients and more water if necessary. Bake for 1 more hour, removing the cover the last 15 or 20 minutes to brown. Add more water if juice has evaporated. Remove meat to platter and make gravy. Serves 8.

MOOSE STROGANOFF

1 1/2 pounds ground moose meat
2 tablespoons minced onion
1/2 tablespoon parsley flakes
1/4 teaspoon garlic powder
1 teaspoon salt
1/4 to 1/2 teaspoon pepper
2/3 cup drained mushrooms
1 can vegetable soup
1 cup sour cream
1/2 cup milk
1 teaspoon poppy seed

Brown meat with onion, parsley, and garlic powder. Stir in salt, pepper, mushrooms, and soup. Simmer 15 minutes. Blend in sour cream and milk. Heat thoroughly. Place in 9-x-9-inch baking dish or 2 1/2-quart casserole. Let stand while preparing Biscuit Topping (below). Serves 6 to 8.

Biscuit Topping

1 1/2 cups sifted flour
2 teaspoons baking powder
1 teaspoon paprika
1/2 teaspoon salt
1/4 teaspoon white pepper
1/2 teaspoon celery seed
1/4 cup shortening
3/4 cup milk

Sift together flour, baking powder, paprika, and salt and pepper. Add celery seed. Cut in shortening until particles are fine. Add milk and stir only until dry particles are moistened. Then drop topping by tablespoons onto meat mixture. Sprinkle with poppy seed, and bake in 475°F. oven 15 to 20 minutes.

CARIBOU COLLOPS

Cut caribou steak about 1/2 inch thick and divide into portions 2 inches square. Season with salt and place in chafing dish or covered frying pan with 2 tablespoons butter. Brown each side as quickly as possible; then add a dust of cayenne, 2 tablespoons port wine, 1 tablespoon currant jelly. Let simmer until inside shows only pink when cut.

BRAISED ELK CHOPS IN MUSHROOM GRAVY

4 good-size loin elk chops
1 3/4 teaspoons salt
1/16 teaspoon pepper
3 tablespoons butter OR margarine
1 cup water
1 can mushroom soup
1 teaspoon sherry
2 drops tabasco

Wipe chops clean with a damp cloth and trim off any fat. Sprinkle with salt and pepper and, using skillet with tight-fitting cover, brown chops slowly (uncovered) on both sides in heated butter. Add 1/4 cup of water, cover, and simmer 15 minutes. Then add 1/4 cup more water and again cover and simmer 15 minutes. Add rest of the water and the soup. Cover and continue cooking very slowly 1/2 hour. Add sherry and tabasco sauce. Serve at once. Serves 4.

ELK BEAUJOLAIS

2 pounds elk meat, cut in strips
3 slices lean bacon
1 clove garlic, crushed
1 pound mushrooms, diced
6 white onions, sliced
3 tablespoons butter
1/3 cup butter
1 cup flour
1 1/2 cans beef consommé
1 1/2 cups beaujolais wine
1 bay leaf
1 tablespoon chopped parsley
salt
thyme
pepper
2 carrots, sliced

Chop bacon and brown in large electric or range skillet; then set bacon aside. Brown elk in bacon drippings, stirring often. Then set skillet containing elk meat aside. Sauté garlic clove, mushrooms, and onions in 3 tablespoons of butter in a separate skillet and set that aside. Melt 1/3 cup butter in original cooking container and add flour. Cook and stir until the flour is a light brown. Then add beef consommé and beaujolais wine, bay leaf, chopped parsley, and sprinkle generously with salt, thyme, and pepper. Add carrots, bacon, mushrooms, onions, elk. Cover and simmer 1 1/2 hours, or until the meat becomes tender. Additional wine may be added, when necessary, to keep meat moist. Serves 6.

ELK SAUERBRATEN

4 to 5 pounds elk chuck, rump,
OR round
salt, pepper
1 onion sliced
3 bay leaves
6 peppercorns
water
vinegar
salt
sugar
1/4 cup brown sugar
1/4 cup raisins
6 gingersnaps

Sprinkle meat with salt and pepper and rub in thoroughly. Place in deep enamel or earthenware dish with onion, bay leaves, and peppercorns. Heat equal parts of water and vinegar; add salt and sugar to taste. Pour hot mixture over meat to cover. Then cover dish and place in refrigerator for 4 to 5 days, turning meat each day. Put meat in deep dutch oven with a little of the spiced vinegar over it. Place in 400°F. oven and brown. Cover tightly and simmer 3 to 4 hours, or until tender. Add more vinegar if necessary. Remove meat, slice as for serving and keep hot. Strain liquid in dutch oven and skim off fat. Let 1/4 cup brown sugar melt in iron skillet and gradually add the strained liquid, then add raisins and gingersnaps. Cook until thickened and smooth. Pour over meat while hot. Serves 10.

HUNTER'S ELK STEAK

4 to 6 medium-size elk steaks
flour
1/2 cup shortening
1 large onion, sliced
2 to 4 cups water
1/4 cup flour
salt
pepper
chili pepper

Pound steaks to tenderize, then roll in flour, and fry in a large skillet until well done or to personal liking. Remove from the skillet and place in a casserole. Use skillet to brown onion. Pour water over the onions and blend in flour. Stir until thick. Season to taste with salt and pepper and chili pepper. Pour over steaks in casserole. Bake in 350°F. oven 30 to 45 minutes. Serves 4 to 6.

Scalloped potatoes go with this.

BROILED ELK STEAK

2 pounds elk steak, cut 1-inch thick
1 clove garlic
2 tablespoons butter OR other fat,
melted
4 large mushroom caps
salt, pepper
parsley
watercress

Wipe steak with a damp, clean cloth. Rub both sides with cut surfaces of garlic and brush with melted butter. Place on a greased broiler rack in a hot broiler and cook 5 minutes. Turn, brush again with butter, and broil an additional 5 to 8 minutes. Broil mushroom caps. Season steak with salt and pepper and garnish with mushroom caps, parsley, and watercress. Serves 4.

TASTY ELK ROAST

4- to 6-pound roast, any cut
2 teaspoons salt
1/4 teaspoon pepper
1 cup mushroom soup
1 envelope onion-soup mix
1 clove garlic, minced
1 pinch rosemary
2 bay leaves
1 tablespoon parsley, snipped
2 tablespoons flour
1/4 cup water

Trim excess fat from meat, season with salt and pepper, and place on sheet of aluminum foil. Pour mushroom soup over and around it. Then sprinkle with onion-soup mix, minced garlic, and rosemary. Add bay leaves. Seal ends of foil tightly leaving 1/2- to 1-inch air space on top. Bake in 350°F. oven. (Bake 30 minutes per pound for shoulder roast and similar cuts. Reduce time to 20 minutes for sirloin and similar cuts.) Remove foil and sprinkle with parsley. Thicken liquid for gravy using 2 tablespoons flour in 1/4 cup water. Venison or antelope may be used in this recipe in place of elk, if desired. Serves 6 to 8.

BEAR

A grown bear of any species is a ponderous animal, and the effort of preparing steaks and roasts can pay off handsomely. Mature bear is generally considered too tough to be palatable, but the haunch or saddle of a young bear is very good when roasted. (See recipe for Saddle of Antelope.) If mature bear meat is used it should be served in a highly seasoned ragout or subjected to a tenderizing process. The old saying: "How they taste depends upon what they've been eating," which applies to some degree to all forms of wild meat, is particularly true of bear. Bear grease, however, is highly prized as a cooking fat. Many hunters consider their winter store of supplies incomplete until they have killed a bear and rendered the clear, sweet lard for cooking.

BEAR LOIN STEAK

2 3/4-inch-thick loin steaks
1 tablespoon butter, melted
2 teaspoons lemon juice
salt, pepper
1/2 cup boiling water

Wipe steaks clean with damp cloth. Trim off *all* fat. Place steak on broiler rack. Brush with butter and lemon juice. Sprinkle with salt and pepper. Broil about 8 minutes. Turn steaks and brush with remaining lemon juice and butter. Salt and pepper. Broil another 8 minutes. Remove from the broiler. Drizzle the 1/2 cup water over the rack and scrape down sides into drip pan. Heat drippings until boiling and pour over hot steaks. Serve immediately.

BEAR STEW

8 pounds bear meat
4 bags carrots
1 bag onions (No. 3 size)
1 stalk celery
1 jigger vinegar (1 1/2 ounces)
4 8-ounce cans mushrooms
dash of garlic salt
salt, pepper

Cut all fat from meat, cube meat into large pieces, and brown. Clean and cube all vegetables and simmer meat with 1/2 of the cleaned carrots, 1/2 of the onions, *all* of the celery, and the jigger of vinegar. When meat and vegetables are cooked, remove carrots, celery, and onions, and discard. Put in remaining carrots and onions and simmer again. Cook until done and add mushrooms. Thicken stew as you would gravy. Season with salt, pepper, garlic salt to taste. Serves 12.

BRAISED BEAR

1 2- to 3-pound bear roast
salt, pepper
1 clove garlic, crushed
2 tablespoons brown sugar
1 tablespoon paprika
1 teaspoon dry mustard
1/4 teaspoon chili powder
1/8 teaspoon cayenne pepper
2 tablespoons worcestershire sauce
1/4 cup vinegar
1 cup tomato juice
1/2 cup water

Place roast in small roaster. Season with salt, pepper, and garlic. Roast in 350°F. oven 1 hour, or until well done. Slice into thin slices. Mix 1 teaspoonful salt with remaining ingredients in heavy skillet. Simmer 15 minutes. Add meat and simmer 1 hour, or until meat is tender. Serves 6 to 8.

BROILED BEAR CHOPS OR STEAKS

Cut chops or steaks from the rump (allow 1 per person), lance them, then marinate them for 24 hours in a mixture of 1 cup olive oil, 1/2 cup lemon juice, 2 tablespoons chopped shallots, 1/2 teaspoon thyme, 1/2 teaspoon basil, black pepper, 1 teaspoon salt, and 2 bay leaves. Wipe meat. Broil on hot charcoal fire or in oven broiler.

POT-ROASTED BEAR IN RED WINE

4 pounds bear meat, choice roast
2 cups dry red wine
1 cup undiluted canned consommé
2 medium-size onions, sliced
2 cloves garlic, chopped
2 bay leaves
2 cloves
1/4 teaspoon oregano
1/4 teaspoon celery seed
1/4 teaspoon fresh cracked white
peppercorns
1 teaspoon salt

Mix all ingredients together, except meat. Then pour marinade over meat and let stand 3 to 4 days in a cool place. Turn meat every day. Take meat out of marinade, drain well. Sear in hot fat until brown on all sides. Put in pan that has a tight cover, pour marinade over meat, and bring to a boil. Simmer in oven or on stove for 2 hours. (Very slow cooking is the trick.) Strain liquid into a bowl. Skim off fat, mix 3 tablespoons of fat with 3 tablespoons flour, add to hot liquid, and cook 2 to 3 minutes. Add salt, if needed. Put meat and gravy back in covered pan until ready to serve. Serves 6 to 8.

BEAR MULLIGAN

Cut bear meat into small pieces, season well, and brown in butter. Place in stewing pot. Pour hot water into skillet and then pour the gravy over the meat, adding enough water to cover meat and the vegetables to be added. Cook very slowly, adding the stewing vegetables at hand (potatoes, carrots, tomatoes, whole onions, turnips, string beans, or others). Simmer for at least 2 hours.

BARBECUED BEAR

Parboil 1 1/2 pounds bear meat, (thawed and boneless) in water, allowing about 10 minutes per pound. Prepare Barbecue Sauce (below) while meat is cooking. Place several rashers of bacon in dutch oven, deep-fat fryer, or large pot, and sauté the parboiled meat on all sides. Add the Barbecue Sauce and simmer with meat over medium heat for at least half an hour, or until tender. Serves 6.

Barbecue Sauce

1/2 cup water
4 ounces tomato sauce
2 medium onions, sliced
1/8 teaspoon garlic powder
2 tablespoons brown sugar
1/4 teaspoon dried mustard
1/8 cup each: lemon juice, vinegar, catsup
1 tablespoon worcestershire sauce

Mix all; simmer 10 minutes.

BEAR MINCEMEAT

3 pounds boned bear meat
1 quart water
1 cup chopped dates
1 cup beef suet, fine chopped
3 1/2 pounds apples, pared, cored, and quartered
1 pound seedless raisins
1 pound white raisins
4 cups orange marmalade
2 quarts cider
2 tablespoons cinnamon
1 teaspoon cloves
1 teaspoon nutmeg
3 tablespoons salt

Simmer meat in water until tender (add more water if needed). Drain. Trim away gristle. Put meat through food chopper, using medium blade. Be sure to have 3 pounds of meat after it is ground. Combine with remaining ingredients in kettle. Mix well, bring to a boil, reduce heat, and simmer 1 1/2 hours, stirring often. This mincemeat can be frozen or canned. To can, pour into hot jars. Adjust lids. Process in pressure canner at 10 pounds pressure (240°F.), pints 60 minutes, quarts 75 minutes. Makes about 10 pints.

MARINATED BEAR STEAK

thick slice of bear loin cut into steaks
1 onion, chopped fine
1 carrot, diced
1 teaspoon paprika
1 cup cider
1 tablespoon lemon juice
1 clove garlic, crushed
1 bay leaf
1/4 teaspoon nutmeg
1/2 teaspoon dry mustard
2 tablespoons orange juice
1 clove garlic, crushed
4 tablespoons butter
1 teaspoon prepared mustard
1/4 teaspoon worcestershire sauce
1/2 teaspoon salt
1/8 teaspoon pepper
1/2 teaspoon paprika
2 tablespoons tomato juice

135

Combine the first 11 ingredients, except the meat, and bring slowly to a boil. Boil 5 minutes, then cool. Use to marinate bear steaks 24 hours in refrigerator. Remove steaks from marinade and sear on both sides in broiler under high heat. Reduce heat and broil, basting often with a mixture of the last 8 ingredients. When steaks are done, dust with salt, pepper, and parsley. Serve with mushrooms sautéed in butter.

MT. SHEEP, MT. GOAT

For butchering instructions, follow those outlined for deer.

Packing out for sheep and goat is usually a tedious business, unless pack horses can be brought to the spot where the animal has been taken. But unfortunately these animals are usually found only at high altitudes and a long way from civilization. In addition, mountain sheep may weigh as much as 300 pounds dressed, and that represents a fair packing problem when the going is steep and the country rough—normal conditions in sheep and goat country. Fortunately the trip is generally all downhill, at least to the point where you can begin to make use of your pack horses or other form of trans-

portation. And you'll discover when you get the animal back to camp, it's been well worth the effort, particularly in the case of the sheep.

The meat of the mountain sheep is tender and excellent in flavor. Mountain goat, on the other hand, is black and strong, and tougher than most big-game meats. Venison recipes may be used for the cooking of both, but the goat will require extra soaking or parboiling.

ROAST MOUNTAIN SHEEP

Prepare roast, wipe, and dry. Place in 350°F. oven, adding enough water for basting. Do not salt until meat begins to roast well. The salt tends to toughen the meat and draw out too much of its juice. About 15 minutes before it is done, dredge the meat very lightly with flour, baste with melted butter, and let brown. Skim the gravy and thicken very slightly with browned flour. Serve with currant, grape, or mint jelly.

ROAST MOUNTAIN GOAT

Soak overnight in vinegar fortified with cloves, cinnamon, mustard, and salt and pepper. Wipe dry, brown in hot fat, then cook 2 hours at 5 to 10 pounds pressure in a pressure cooker. Thirty minutes before meat is done add seasoned vegetables.

ANTELOPE

Antelope are found on rolling country or wide open plains and are relatively small animals, averaging about 80 pounds, dressed, which makes carrying them back to camp an easy task. For butchering instructions, follow those given for deer. Antelope meat is slightly gamier than venison.

ANTELOPE STEAK DELUXE

2 pounds steak, 1-inch thick, cut in serving pieces
2 tablespoons shortening
4 tablespoons flour
2 soup cans water
salt, pepper
can cream of mushroom soup
1 cup diced celery
1/4 cup diced onions
can mushroom slices, drained

Heat shortening in skillet, pound flour into meat, and brown well. Put in 1 can water and simmer for half an hour. Add salt and pepper. Pour on soup and remaining water, mixed together. Add celery, onions, and mushrooms, and cook on low heat for 1 hour. Serves 6.

Fluffy riced potatoes, with snipped parsley for color, and shoepeg corn with pimiento round out the meal.

CHARCOAL-BROILED ANTELOPE STEAK

antelope steaks
red wine
melted butter

Cut steaks 1-inch thick and trim off fat. Soak in red wine 5 to 10 minutes. Drain off wine and spread steaks with melted butter. Broil over charcoal fire, turning occasionally, and spread on more melted butter. Continue until cooked to your taste.

SADDLE OF ANTELOPE

Clean and lard a saddle of antelope. Sprinkle it with salt and pepper and rub well with flour. Place on rack in pan, roast in 450°F. oven half an hour, and then reduce heat to 300°F. and cook for 1 1/2 to 2 hours longer. Do not add water to pan. If fat covering is very thin, put several strips of bacon on top for basting. Serve with currant jelly sauce.

POTTED ANTELOPE STEAK

1 1 1/2-inch-thick antelope steak
flour
salt pepper
dry mustard
milk
1/2 cup sliced onions
1/2 cup chopped celery

Pound steak in flour to which salt, pepper, and dry mustard have been added. Put floured steak into dutch oven in hot fat and brown. Add milk to cover steak. Then add sliced onions and chopped celery and simmer 1 hour. Thicken pot gravy with flour to the thickness desired.

HONEY ANTELOPE BAKE

1 large antelope steak, about
3 inches thick
1/2 cup flour
1/8 pound butter
3 cups sour cream
1/4 teaspoon monosodium
glutamate
1/2 teaspoon salt
1/8 teaspoon freshly ground pepper
1/4 cup honey

Knead flour into steak, and brown it well in butter. Cover bottom of baking pan with 1 1/2 cups sour cream. Add steak and season. Pour honey over top. Cover and bake in 250°F. oven 1 1/2 hours, or until tender. Add more sour cream, when necessary, to retain moistness. Serves 4.

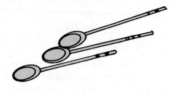

HUNTER'S STEW

2 pounds chuck of any big game,
cut in pieces
3 tablespoons salad oil
2 cloves garlic, minced
3 large onions, quartered
1 6-ounce can tomato paste
1 tablespoon flour
1 teaspoon chili powder
1 teaspoon oregano
1 teaspoon rosemary
1 1/2 tablespoons seasoned salt
2 16-ounce cans stewed tomatoes
1/2 cup snipped celery OR parsley
1 cup water
3 medium carrots
1/2 pound macaroni
1/2 cup shredded parmesan cheese

In large dutch oven heat salad oil and brown meat on all sides. Add garlic and onion and sauté well, turning frequently. Stir in tomato paste, flour, chili powder, oregano, rosemary, seasoned salt, tomatoes, and celery or parsley. Add water and simmer, covered, 1 hour and 15 minutes. Skim off fat if necessary. Add carrots and simmer 45 minutes longer. Meanwhile, cook macaroni, as package directs. Drain it well and stir into stew with parmesan. Serves 6.

Serve with a tossed green salad and crisp bread, such as homemade corn crisps. For dessert, add an old-fashioned sweet—Blueberry Fool or Indian Pudding with ice cream.

BIG-GAME CASSEROLE

1 1/2 pounds ground big game
1 cup chopped onion
1/4 teaspoon pepper
1 teaspoon salt
shortening
1 can condensed cream of mushroom
soup
1 7-ounce package elbow macaroni
1 cup dairy sour cream
2 tablespoons sherry (optional)
1 17-ounce can sweet peas, drained

Combine ground meat, onion, and seasoning, shape into small meatballs, and brown in a little shortening. Stir in soup, cover, and simmer 10 minutes. Remove from heat. Meanwhile, cook macaroni according to package directions. Stir in sour cream, sherry, macaroni, and peas into meat mixture. Pour into a 2 1/2-quart casserole and bake in 350°F. oven 35 minutes.

BOAR

Boar is wild pig, and the flavor is deliciously pork-like. However, unless the boar is a young one, the meat will not be as tender as pork from the butcher's—it will need slow, moist cooking for best results. But those results are worth every effort to obtain them, for boar, properly cooked, is a delicacy.

SADDLE OF BOAR

Season the saddle of a young boar with salt and pepper; sprinkle with thyme. Roast uncovered in a 325°F. oven 35 minutes per pound, basting with pan drippings. Make gravy, if desired. Serve with yams and fresh, hot applesauce.

POT ROAST OF BOAR

boar shoulder roast
salted water to cover
2 cups water
3 cups apple cider
2 onions, sliced
2 carrots, sliced
1/2 cup sliced celery
1/2 teaspoon dry sage

Simmer meat in salted water to cover for 1 1/2 hours. Drain and return to kettle with remaining ingredients. Cover and simmer until tender. Slice meat and arrange on hot platter to keep warm. Make gravy from cooking liquid. Serve with buttered noodles.

BOAR SPARERIBS WITH SAUERKRAUT

Cover bottom of roasting pan with sauerkraut. Place over it 3 strips of bacon, diced, 2 apples, sliced. Place boar ribs on top, sprinkle with salt and pepper. Bake in 350°F. oven for 1 1/2 hours. Serve with sautéed parsnips.

ACCOMPANIMENTS
FOR GAME

What to have with your game dinner should never be a problem. Simply think back to our ancestors, whose main source of meat was what they acquired hunting. Vegetables, such as beans, mushrooms, succotash, corn custard, squash—both the summer and winter varieties—brussels sprouts (try them with chestnuts), fried tomatoes, fried parsnips, sweet-sour red cabbage, peas, turnips and rutabagas, onions, Jerusalem artichokes, beet greens with a few baby beets pulled along with them—all of these are good with a meal based on game.

Bread? There are buttermilk biscuits, beaten biscuits, anadama bread, sourdough, cornbread in its many varieties, Sally Lunn, blueberry or cranberry muffins, sweet-potato rolls, to name just a few. And sourdough! Sourdough and game were made for each other. Bring on fresh comb honey with these breads.

Side dishes? How about potato pancakes, mashed potato cakes, sweet potatoes or yams, spoonbread made with stone-ground cornmeal, rice cooked almost any way, wild rice—of course!—hominy and hominy grits, and homemade noodles?

Desserts? Try gingerbread, pound cake, butternut or hickory nut cake, Gooseberry Fool, Blueberry Slump, cranberry pie, Indian pudding— gilded with a ball of vanilla ice cream—persimmon pudding, cottage pudding with lemon sauce, deep-dish apple or berry pies, homemade maple walnut or black walnut ice cream, and old-fashioned soft custard, dressed up into a floating island.

But most important of all to the serving of game is the choice of a just-right stuffing and/or sauce and/or relish to serve with the meat. Try some of these.

PARSLEY JELLY

Sterilize 4 8-ounce jelly glasses and let stand in the hot water. Sterilize 4 teaspoons. Put 2 firmly packed cups parsley, washed and stems removed, in a large saucepan and crush parsley well, using potato masher or large pestle. Pour 2 1/4 cups cold water over the parsley and bring to boiling point. Remove from heat, cover, and let stand 15 minutes. Strain through cheesecloth. Measure 1 1/2 cups of the parsley water and combine it in a large saucepan with: 2 tablespoons lemon juice, 3 or 4 drops green food coloring, and 2 1/2 cups sugar. Mix well and bring to a rolling boil over high heat. Stir in 1/2 of a 6-ounce bottle of liquid pectin. Bring again to a rolling boil, stirring constantly, and boil 1 minute. Remove from heat and skim. In each prepared jelly glass, put a large sprig parsley. Ladle in jelly. Weigh down sprig of parsley against bottom of glass with sterilized spoon. Let stand 20 minutes. Take spoons out carefully. Cover jelly with 1/8-inch hot paraffin. Cool. Cover with lids.

POACHED APPLES

5 cooking apples
1 cup sugar
2 cups water
1/4 teaspoon salt
5 or 6 drops red food coloring
1/2 teaspoon cinnamon extract
1/4 teaspoon nutmeg extract
1 teaspoon vanilla

Pare the apples and cut them in half crosswise. Pick out seeds, but do not core. Make a syrup of remaining ingredients in a large skillet and bring to a boil. Slip in the apples and simmer until tender—

watch carefully, lest they get too tender all at once. If nutmeg and cinnamon flavoring extracts are not obtainable, use the same amounts of the dry spice; mix with the 1 cup sugar before adding to water.

CANDIED CRANBERRIES

2 cups fresh cranberries
1 cup sugar

Spread cranberries in single layer in bottom of a shallow baking dish. Sprinkle sugar over. Cover dish tightly with foil. Bake in 350°F. oven 1 hour, stirring three times during baking and re-covering after each stirring. Refrigerate. Serve with any wild fowl.

SPICY PRUNES

Rinse 1 pound large prunes, cover with cold water, and cook 10 to 12 minutes. Drain. Combine 1 cup vinegar, 1 cup sugar, 1 cup water, 1 teaspoon ground cloves, 1 teaspoon cinnamon. Boil 1 minute. Add prunes and bring to boil. Cool and refrigerate. Make relish at least 1 week before using it.

ORANGE-GLAZED APPLES

4 red-skinned cooking apples
2 teaspoons grated orange rind
1/2 cup orange juice
1/2 cup sugar

Quarter apples and core them, but do not pare. Combine orange rind, orange juice, and granulated sugar in a skillet and place apples, skin side up, in mixture. Simmer, covered, over low heat 10 to 15 minutes, or until apples are tender, but still hold their shape. Take out apple pieces, continue to cook sauce until thickened and spoon over apples. Serve with any game fowl.

PICKLED ENGLISH WALNUTS

Walnuts should be gathered when the nut is soft enough that a pin can be easily stuck into it. Pour boiling salted water over the nuts and let stand 3 days. Change salted water and let stand another 3 days longer. Change once more and let stand another 3 days. Drain nuts and place them in a single layer on plates, turning several times, until they turn dark. Put into jars or crock. For each 20 nuts add: 1 clove garlic, crushed; 8 whole cloves; 1/2 teaspoon mustard seed, 10 whole peppercorns, 1 teaspoon dried horseradish, and cover completely with cold cider vinegar.

GINGER PEARS

2 large cans pear halves
10 whole cloves
2 2-inch pieces, stick cinnamon
1/4 teaspoon nutmeg
4 teaspoons lemon juice
1 teaspoon grated lemon rind
1 teaspoon grated orange rind
2 1/2 tablespoons crystallized
ginger, chopped
1/8 teaspoon ground ginger
2 tablespoons butter

Drain pears and reserve syrup. In medium saucepan, combine 1 1/2 cups reserved syrup with spices and bring to a boil. Reduce heat and simmer, uncovered, 5 minutes. Remove cloves and discard. Then add lemon juice, lemon and orange rind and remaining ingredients. Simmer, uncovered, stirring occasionally, 15 to 20 minutes, or until slightly thickened. Serve hot.

FRESH PEACH CHUTNEY

8 cups peaches, peeled and cut up
1 medium onion
1 small clove garlic
1 cup seedless raisins
2 tablespoons chili powder
1 cup crystallized ginger, chopped
2 tablespoons mustard seed
1 tablespoon salt
1 quart vinegar
2 1/4 cups light-brown sugar,
firmly packed

Peel and cut up peaches, enough to make 8 cups. Sterilize 5 pint jars and leave in hot water until ready to fill. Put onion, garlic, and raisins through fine blade of food chopper. Then mix spices into ground mixture. Combine with peaches and remaining ingredients in large kettle and mix well. Bring to boiling point, stirring constantly until sugar is dissolved. Reduce heat and simmer, uncovered, stirring occasionally, about 45 to 60 minutes. Ladle chutney into hot, sterilized jars.

SPICY CONCORD JELLY

2 6-ounce cans frozen grape
juice concentrate, thawed
6 1/2 cups sugar
1/2 teaspoon cinnamon
1/2 teaspoon cloves
1/2 teaspoon allspice
3 cups water
1 6-ounce bottle liquid pectin

Sterilize 10 8-ounce jelly glasses and leave in hot water. In large kettle, combine sugar and spices with water and mix well. Cook over high heat, stirring constantly, until sugar is dissolved. Bring to a rolling boil, stirring constantly, then boil hard 1 minute, continuing to stir. Remove from heat. Stir in grape juice concentrate and pectin, mixing well. Ladle into hot, sterilized jelly glasses. Immediately cover with 1/8-inch hot paraffin.

PORT-WINE JELLY

2 cups port wine
3 cups sugar
1/8 teaspoon cinnamon
1/8 teaspoon cloves
1/2 6-ounce bottle liquid fruit pectin

Sterilize 4 8-ounce jelly glasses and leave in hot water. In top of double-boiler, combine port, sugar, cinnamon, and cloves. Place over rapidly boiling water and heat 2 minutes, stirring constantly. Then, over direct heat, bring to a rolling boil and stir in pectin. Again bring to a rolling boil and boil 1 minute, stirring constantly. Remove from heat. Skim off foam. Ladle jelly into hot glasses. Cover immediately with 1/8-inch hot paraffin. Let cool and cover with lid.

SPEEDY CORN RELISH

2 cups drained canned OR cooked
frozen whole-kernel corn
1/4 cup chopped green pepper
1/2 medium onion, sliced thin
6 tablespoons sweet-pickle relish
with liquid
1/4 teaspoon celery seeds
1/2 teaspoon salt
1/4 teaspoon dry mustard
2 tablespoons vinegar
1 tablespoon brown sugar
1 tablespoon water

In saucepan, combine all ingredients and simmer 5 minutes. Refrigerate until ready to serve.

TOMATO RELISH

2 pounds tomatoes
2 green peppers
2 medium onions
1/2 cup fine-chopped celery
2 teaspoons salt
1 teaspoon dry mustard
1/4 cup vinegar
1/4 cup olive oil
1/2 teaspoon salt
1/2 teaspoon sugar

Seed peppers and chop together with tomatoes and onions. Add celery, then remaining ingredients, and mix well. Refrigerate until ready to serve—at least 3 hours to blend flavors.

JELLIED APRICOT RELISH

1 large can apricot halves
1/4 cup vinegar
1/2 cup sugar
12 cloves
1 2-inch stick cinnamon
1 3-ounce package orange-flavored gelatin

Drain syrup from apricots into saucepan and add vinegar, sugar, and spices. Bring to a boil. Add apricots and simmer 10 minutes. Remove apricots to 6 individual molds or custard cups. Strain syrup and add enough hot water to make 2 cups. Pour over gelatin and stir until dissolved. Then pour over apricots. Refrigerate overnight.

ORANGE-CRANBERRY JELLY

1 quart cranberry juice
6 cups sugar
peel from 1 orange
1 6-ounce bottle liquid pectin

Sterilize 8 8-ounce jelly glasses and leave in hot water. Then in large saucepan, combine cranberry juice and sugar. Peel 1 orange, leaving the peel in large pieces to be tied in a small, double thickness of cheesecloth. Add peel in cheesecloth bag to cranberry mixture. Stir, over high heat, until sugar is dissolved. Then bring mixture to a rolling boil. Stir in liquid pectin and again bring to a rolling boil. Boil 1 minute, stirring constantly. Remove from heat. Remove orange peel in cheesecloth bag and skim off foam. Ladle jelly into hot glasses. Cover immediately with 1/8-inch hot paraffin. Let cool and cover with lid.

SPICED CRANBERRIES

4 cups fresh cranberries
1 1/2 cups water
2 3-inch pieces cinnamon stick
6 whole cloves
5 whole allspice
3 cups sugar

Wash cranberries, drain, and remove stems. Turn into 3 1/2-quart saucepan. Add water. Tie spices in double thickness of cheesecloth and add to saucepan. Cover pan and cook over medium heat until cranberries burst, about 10 minutes. Turn heat low. Remove and discard cheesecloth bag. Stir in sugar and cook, stirring constantly, 5 minutes. Cool and refrigerate.

BREAD SAUCE

1/3 cup fine stale breadcrumbs
1 onion
6 cloves
2 cups milk
1/2 teaspoon salt
few grains of cayenne
3 tablespoons butter
1/2 cup coarse stale breadcrumbs

Add *fine* breadcrumbs and the onion stuck with cloves to the milk in a double-boiler and scald for 30 minutes. Then remove onion and add salt, cayenne pepper, and 2 tablespoons of butter. Brown coarse crumbs in remaining butter and sprinkle on sauce.

HOT ORANGE SAUCE

2/3 cup orange juice
1/4 cup butter
1/4 cup flour
1/2 teaspoon salt
few grains of cayenne
1 1/3 cups of brown stock
2 tablespoons sherry OR port
grated rind of 1 orange

Melt butter and add flour and seasonings, stirring until well browned. Slowly add stock and simmer a few minutes. Just before serving, add orange juice, wine, and orange rind.

COLD ORANGE SAUCE

grated rind of 2 oranges
6 tablespoons currant jelly
2 tablespoons orange juice
3 tablespoons sugar
2 tablespoons lemon juice
1/4 teaspoon salt
dash of cayenne
2 tablespoons port

Put grated orange rind, jelly, and sugar in bowl and beat well. Add remaining ingredients and stir until blended thoroughly.

PORT-WINE SAUCE

1 cup port wine
1/2 cup orange juice
1 small onion, diced
1/2 teaspoon dried thyme
1 cup chicken OR game stock
2 teaspoons cornstarch
orange sections
grated orange rind
salt, pepper

Combine wine and orange juice and simmer onion and thyme in the mixture. When liquid has been reduced by half, add the stock. Mix cornstarch with a little water, stir

145

into liquid, and cook until sauce is thick and hot. Add orange sections and rind and season to taste.

CHESTNUT SAUCE

1 cup cooked chestnuts
3 tablespoons butter
3 tablespoons flour
1 cup milk
1/2 cup heavy cream
salt, pepper
dash of nutmeg

Whirl chestnuts in blender, or grate, or chop very fine. Next make cream sauce using butter, flour, milk, and heavy cream. Season with salt and pepper and freshly grated nutmeg. Combine nuts and sauce and heat through.

WILD GRAPE SAUCE

4 cups wild grapes
4 tablespoons butter
1/4 cup sherry
3 whole cloves
1 tablespoon lemon juice
1 tablespoon grated lemon rind

Wash grapes, cover with boiling water, and simmer 5 minutes. Drain. Put through a sieve. Melt butter in a saucepan and add sherry, cloves, and lemon juice. Simmer 5 minutes. Remove cloves and add grape purée and lemon rind. Heat through. Serve with any game bird.

SAUCE ROBERT

Brown 3/4 cup of chopped onion in 1/4 cup of butter. Add a can of beef gravy, 1 tablespoon wine vinegar, 1/2 cup dry white wine, 1 tablespoon brown prepared mustard, and salt and pepper to taste. Particularly good with goose and turkey.

SAUCE POIVRADE

3 tablespoons olive oil
1/3 cup chopped carrot
1/3 cup chopped onion
4 tablespoons minced parsley
1 cup dry red wine
2 1/2 cups canned beef gravy
1/8 teaspoon ground cloves
1 1/2 teaspoons fresh-ground black pepper

Pour oil in skillet and heat. Then sauté carrot, onion, and parsley about 5 minutes. Add wine and simmer until reduced by half. Add gravy and cook over low heat about half an hour. Strain. Place in a saucepan and stir in cloves and pepper. Simmer 5 minutes. This is one of the traditional sauces to serve with venison.

GREEK LEMON SAUCE

juice of 1 large lemon
3 eggs, separated
salt
2 cups chicken broth

Beat egg whites and yolks separately, then together until they are blended. Gradually beat in lemon juice and 2 cups of boiling chicken broth. Heat, but do not boil—boiling will cause curdling. Very good with light-meat game birds.

HUNTER'S SAUCE

4 tablespoons butter
2 medium onions, chopped
3 tomatoes, peeled, seeded,
and diced
6 large mushroom caps, sliced thin
2 cups game stock
2 tablespoons flour
1/4 cup red wine

Melt 2 tablespoons butter in a deep skillet and sauté onions until transparent. Add tomatoes and mushrooms. Blend in stock and simmer 1 hour, stirring occasionally. Meanwhile, blend the flour into 2 remaining tablespoons butter, creaming together well. Just before serving sauce, thicken with this flour-butter roux, add wine, blend well, and heat through.

SALMI SAUCE

Combine juice and grated rind of 2 oranges with 1/4 cup of port wine and 2 cups of canned beef gravy. Simmer for a few minutes to blend and reduce slightly. Excellent with all kinds of game.

CHERRY SAUCE

1/2 pound Bing cherries, pitted
1/4 cup minced onions
1/4 cup butter
1 tablespoon flour
2 cans consommé
1/3 cup sherry
2 tablespoons brandy

Pit cherries and set aside. Then cook onions in butter until wilted. Stir in flour and cook a few minutes. Meanwhile boil consommé until reduced to half of original quantity. Add to onions. Add sherry and brandy and cook 5 minutes. Add cherries and heat through. Use with any big game other than bear, or with wild duck or woodcock.

MINT-CURRANT SAUCE

1 cup currant jelly
2 tablespoons chopped mint leaves
2 tablespoons grated orange rind

With fork, break jelly. Mix in chopped mint leaves and grated orange rind. Goes well with duck— or, as a change, with venison.

CUMBERLAND SAUCE

1/2 cup currant jelly
1 grated rind lemon and juice
1 grated orange rind
1 tablespoon confectioners sugar
1 teaspoon prepared mustard
1 tablespoon port wine

Melt jelly over low heat. Stir in remaining ingredients and heat through. Cumberland is one of the traditional sauces for venison, but it's also delicious with ham.

CREAM SAUCE FOR SMALL GAME BIRDS

After roasting small game birds, flame in 1 tablespoon brandy for each bird. Remove birds and keep warm. Pour off the pan juices and reduce over low heat 1 minute. Then add 1 egg yolk for each bird and beat in 1/2 cup heavy cream. Stir until thickened, but do not boil. Season to taste.

FLUFFY HORSERADISH SAUCE

1 8-ounce package cream cheese
1 tablespoon confectioners sugar
1 tablespoon lemon juice
1 tablespoon worcestershire sauce
2 tablespoons prepared horseradish
1/2 cup heavy cream

Soften cream cheese to room temperature. Blend in remaining ingredients, except the cream. Whip cream and fold into cream cheese mixture.

CELERY SAUCE FOR PARTRIDGE

Wash and dice a large bunch of celery. Simmer in enough water to cover until tender, then add 1 cup cream, 1/4 teaspoon mace, 1/4 teaspoon nutmeg. Take 2 table-spoons butter and roll in flour. Add to celery mixture and simmer. Serve with roasted partridge or other game birds.

ORANGE SAUCE FOR WILD DUCK

3 tablespoons butter
duck liver
3 tablespoons cognac
2 teaspoons minced shallot
1 tablespoon grated lemon rind
3 tablespoons flour
1/8 teaspoon pepper
1/2 teaspoon tomato paste
1 teaspoon meat-extract paste
1/2 cup orange juice
1 cup canned chicken broth
1/4 cup claret
1/4 cup orange marmalade
3 large oranges, sectioned

Heat butter in medium skillet. Add liver and brown well. Add brandy, shallot, and lemon rind and simmer 3 minutes. Remove from heat. Remove liver, chop fine, and reserve. Into same skillet, stir flour, pepper, tomato paste, and meat-extract paste. Gradually add orange juice, broth, claret, and marmalade. Bring to boil. Reduce heat and simmer, stirring, 15 min-utes. Add orange sections and chopped liver. Serve hot. Makes about 3 cups.

SWEET-SOUR MUSTARD SAUCE

3 tablespoons prepared mustard
1 egg
1/3 cup light brown sugar, firmly packed
1 teaspoon paprika
1/2 cup cider vinegar
1 tablespoon butter

In small bowl, combine mustard, egg, sugar, and paprika. Beat with rotary beater. Add vinegar and beat again. Melt butter in small saucepan, take from heat, and allow to cool. Blend mixed ingredients into cooled butter. Cook, stirring, over low heat, until thickened, about 4 to 5 minutes. Cool.

CREAM GRAVY FOR GAME

1 1/2 cups heavy cream
2 teaspoons minced onion
2 tablespoons butter
2 teaspoons flour
2 teaspoons lemon juice
2 teaspoons tart jelly
salt

Pour off fat from pan in which venison or other game has been roasted. Stir in onion, butter, and flour and cook about 2 minutes. Slowly add cream and cook, stirring, until blended and thickened. Add lemon juice and jelly, and cook until melted. Taste. Season if necessary.

SWEET-SOUR SAUCE FOR VENISON

2 tablespoons fat and pan drippings
1 teaspoon minced shallot
1 tablespoon flour
2 tablespoons vinegar
2 cups burgundy
salt, pepper
2 tablespoons currant jelly

After removing cooked venison from pan, pour off all fat and drippings. Return 2 tablespoons fat and drippings to pan and add minced shallot. Add flour and blend well. Add vinegar and wine and cook, stirring, until reduced to half. Taste and season. Stir in currant jelly. Pour over venison.

SAVORY BREAD STUFFING

2 cups fine breadcrumbs
1 small onion, minced
1/4 cup celery and leaves, minced
4 tablespoons butter
1 tablespoon minced parsley
1 teaspoon dried summer savory
1/4 teaspoon salt
dash white pepper
chicken OR other stock

Place breadcrumbs in a bowl. Sauté onion and celery in melted butter 5 minutes. Add (including all butter) to crumbs, along with parsley and seasonings. Use just enough stock to moisten lightly. Will stuff 1 small fowl.

CIDER SAUCE

3/4 cup cider
2 tablespoons butter
1/3 cup flour
1 1/2 cups broth OR water
1/2 cup apple jelly

Melt butter, add flour, and blend. Add broth or water, stir, and bring to boil. Add cider and jelly and bring to boil. Makes approximately 2 cups sauce.

OYSTER STUFFING

1 cup stewing oysters, chopped
4 cups stale bread cubes
2 teaspoons salt
1/8 teaspoon pepper
1/8 teaspoon sage
3 tablespoons butter
1 onion, minced
2 tablespoons minced parsley
3/4 cup minced celery

Place chopped oysters in frying pan, cover, and sauté 5 minutes. Then drain. Combine bread cubes, salt, pepper, and sage, and add oysters. Melt butter in frying pan and add onion, parlsey, and celery. Sauté until tender, add to bread mixture, and blend. Will stuff a 4-pound fowl.

POTATO STUFFING

2 cups hot mashed potatoes
1 1/2 cups breadcrumbs
1 medium onion, chopped
2 eggs, lightly beaten
1 1/2 teaspoons salt
1 teaspoon thyme
1/2 cup chopped celery leaves
1/4 cup chopped parsley

Combine all ingredients and use to stuff an 8- to 9-pound goose.

SOUTHERN-STYLE STUFFING

1/3 cup butter
1/2 cup minced onion
1/4 cup minced green pepper
1/4 cup minced celery
4 cups day-old white breadcrumbs
4 cups crumbled cornbread (made without sugar)
2/3 cup game OR chicken stock
1/2 pound fresh pork-sausage links, cut up
1/4 teaspoon salt
1/8 teaspoon pepper
1/2 teaspoon sage
2 eggs, beaten
1/2 cup chopped walnuts

Melt butter in skillet and saute onion, green pepper, and celery until tender. Place both kinds of breadcrumbs in a large bowl and pour stock over. Add sautéed vegetables. Brown sausage pieces in skillet. Add seasonings, eggs, and walnuts to crumb mixture and mix well. Add sausage and sausage drippings. Will stuff a 10- to 12-pound turkey or several smaller birds.

GOOSE STUFFING ALSACE

1 package poultry stuffing
1 cup mashed cooked chestnuts
2 egg yolks
1/2 cup pitted dates
1/2 cup pitted prunes
1/4 cup chopped almonds
1/4 cup Grand Marnier
1/4 cup orange juice
1 teaspoon Bell's seasoning

Mix all ingredients lightly together in a bowl. When thoroughly mixed, stuff goose. If any stuffing remains, place in baking bowl and heat in oven 30 minutes before goose is removed. This stuffing is also delicious with wild turkey.

CHESTNUT-APPLE STUFFING

2 cans water-packed chestnuts
1/4 cup butter
1 cup chopped celery
1/2 cup chopped onion
1/2 cup raisins
4 cups apples, chopped, pared, and cored
6 cups fresh white-bread cubes
1 tablespoon salt
1 teaspoon cinnamon
1/4 teaspoon nutmeg

Drain chestnuts and chop coarsely. Melt butter in large skillet and sauté celery and onion in it until tender. Lightly toss onion and celery with remaining ingredients in large bowl until well combined. Will stuff a 10- to 12-pound turkey, or 2 to 3 smaller birds.

NUT-RICE STUFFING WITH MUSHROOMS

2/3 cup chopped toasted almonds
2 2/3 cups packaged precooked rice
1 pound mushrooms, sliced thin
1/2 cup chopped onions
2 1/2 cups diced celery with leaves
2 teaspoons salt
1/8 teaspoon pepper
1/2 teaspoon marjoram
1/4 teaspoon thyme
1/2 cup butter
2 1/2 cups water

Add mushrooms, onions, celery, and seasonings to melted butter in large saucepan. Sauté, stirring, until onions are golden. Mix in water and rice. Bring to boil over high heat and simmer 2 minutes, gently fluffing rice once or twice. Taste for seasoning. Add almonds, remove from heat. Will stuff a 6- to 7-pound turkey, or 2 smaller birds.

The flavor of this stuffing may be varied by the substitution of pecans for the almonds, sage for the marjoram and thyme.

151

SOURDOUGH COOKERY

Sourdough bread—and biscuits, flapjacks, muffins and waffles—is a great accompaniment for game of any kind. Such bread has a taste and a consistency unlike those of other "raised" baking that seems somehow just right to round out a wild game meal. And, of course, there's a plus to sourdough baking—once you have achieved a good starter you need no further leavening for future batches of bread, as long as you remember to conserve thriftily some of the starter for next time. Perfect for camping trips and other kinds of outdoor meal preparation, sourdough cookery does not require new yeast each time a baking begins.

Early sourdough starters, usually containing wild yeasts as well as a multitude of bacteria, were very much a by-guess and by-gosh proposition. If desirable organisms won the bacterial war, the starter was a success; if not, an inferior product resulted or the whole production had to be started afresh. But today we can control fermentation to a great extent and expect uniformly good results.

SOURDOUGH STARTER

In making sourdough starter,

you are actually growing your own yeast. Make your first batch of starter at home and carry it to the campsite—then, by saving a part each time you bake, you'll have enough to carry you through the trip. Here's how:

2 cups flour
2 cups lukewarm water
1 yeast cake OR
1 package dry yeast

Mix the three ingredients thoroughly. Let the mixture set overnight in a warm place free from drafts. In the morning the starter should be bubbly and smell nicely yeasty.

Keep the starter in a well-washed and scalded glass or pottery container—metal should never come in contact with it. As far as possible, keep the starter in a cool spot. (If you want to store it for a long time, freeze it.)

To carry the starter to camp easily and safely, work in enough flour to solidify the sponge into a dry clump of dough. Pack this in the middle of the flour you are taking along. Later, water and warmth will reactivate the yeast.

Sometimes starters lose their ability to leaven—particularly if they have been in a warm place too long. If this happens, try adding two tablespoons of unpasteurized cider vinegar, or of cultured or unpasteurized buttermilk or sour cream. (But it doesn't hurt to carry an extra package of fresh-dated dry yeast with you, should all else fail!)

SOURDOUGH BREAD

To your starter, add enough flour and lukewarm water—equal amounts of each—to give you a total of about 3 cups of mixture. Let this stand in a warm place overnight—or, at least, for 6 to 8 hours. Take out two cups of this sponge to use for your baking and put the rest aside—that's your starter for next time.

4 cups flour
2 tablespoons sugar
1 teaspoon salt
2 tablespoons shortening, melted

Mix together the flour, sugar and salt. Make a well in the center of the mixture and pour in the melted shortening. Put the 2 cups of sponge into the well and mix with shortening, then blend well with the flour mixture. You should have a soft dough. If not, add flour or liquid—water or milk. Knead for 3 or 4 minutes on any clean, floured surface. Cut off chunks of the dough to fit the pans you are going to use, and put in a warm place to rise. When doubled in bulk, bake 50 to 60 minutes in a moderately hot oven or reflector baker—preferably one that is hottest in the first 15 minutes. Test with a straw—if it comes out dry, the bread is done.

BEATEN SOURDOUGH BREAD

This is made by the previous method except that instead of kneading the bread, beat it in the mixing bowl for two minutes, then let it rise in the bowl. When it is bubbly, add one teaspoon baking soda and mix for another minute. Turn into a well-greased pan and let stand 10 minutes in a warm place before baking.

SOURDOUGH FLAPJACKS

Add two cups of flour and 2 cups of lukewarm water to sourdough starter and leave to rise overnight in a warm, draft-free place. In the morning take out the original amount of starter and save it.

2 eggs (fresh or dried)
1/2 teaspoon salt
1 tablespoon sugar
1 teaspoon soda
1 teaspoon warm water
2 tablespoons shortening
(melted or liquid)

Mix eggs, salt and sugar with a fork. Dissolve soda in water. Stir egg mixture, dissolved soda and shortening into sourdough batter. If the batter is too thick to pour, thin it with a little milk. Grease a hot griddle or frying pan lightly with bacon rind. Pour out flapjacks; turn

153

when starting to show small bubbles. Turn only once; the second side should take only half as long as the first to cook.

SOURDOUGH MUFFINS

Set the sponge the night before; in the morning take out starter.

1 1/2 cups whole wheat flour
1/2 cup sugar
1 teaspoon salt
1/4 cup dry milk powder
1 1/2 teaspoons baking soda
1 cup raisins (optional)
1/2 cup shortening
(melted or liquid)
2 eggs

Mix together flour, sugar, salt, milk powder and soda. Add raisins—or wild blueberries if you have them. Make a well in the center of these dry ingredients and mix the shortening, egg and sponge in it. Stir into dry ingredients, just enough to blend. Pour into greased muffin tins and bake in a hot oven or reflector baker 20 minutes, or until they are done when tested with a straw.

SOURDOUGH FRENCH BREAD

1 cup water
1/4 cup milk
4 cups flour
2 teaspoons salt

2 tablespoons sugar
1 1/2 tablespoons shortening
(melted or liquid)
1 1/2 cups sourdough starter

Bring the water to a boil; mix with milk. Cool to lukewarm. Mix together flour, salt and sugar in a large bowl. Make a well; into the well put the lukewarm liquid, the shortening and the sourdough starter. Mix together, then mix into dry ingredients for a soft dough. Do not knead. Cover and let rise in a warm, draft-free place until double in bulk—about 2 hours. Turn onto a lightly floured surface. Roll half of dough into a large rectangle. Fold the two long sides toward the middle, then roll like a jelly roll. Repeat with the other half of dough. Grease a large baking sheet and sprinkle with 2 tablespoons cornmeal and place the loaves on it, with smooth side up. Using a sharp knife, make diagonal slits every two inches across top of each loaf. Mix 1 teaspoon cornstarch with 1 teaspoon cold water. Boil 1/2 cup water and add cornstarch mixture. Cool. Brush loaves with the mixture. Cover and let rise again until double in bulk—about 1 hour. Brush the loaves again with cornstarch mixture. Bake 15 minutes in a hot oven or reflector baker. Brush the loaves again with cornstarch mixture. Reduce heat to moderate and continue baking 30 minutes until done and golden brown.

SMOKING AND SMOKE COOKING WILD GAME

I f you have never tasted smoked venison, wild turkey, wild duck, pheasant or quail, there is a pleasant surprise in store for you, for smoking and smoke cooking develop delicate and tantalizing flavors in the game you have taken.

The principle of smoking game is not new and the process is quite simple. Even the beginner will produce tasty food with his first attempt.

Brining of the flesh before the smoking process is started is essential. Two methods of brining are used, the wet and the dry method. The former is more often used, because the wet brining will produce a properly brined product more quickly. This is especially true when you are going to use the hot smoking method to prepare your game. Brining will draw moisture from the flesh of the game to aid in drying the finished product, and it also helps inhibit bacterial growth.

There are two accepted methods of preparing a brine solution of proper salt concentration. Use Morton's Special Salt for canning, pickling and preserving. It is pure salt—nothing added—and is readily obtainable in most grocery stores. Use a stoneware jar or porcelain container without chips or breaks, or a good stainless-steel container. Place your meat in, packing it carefully. Then pour fresh, clean water over the meat until it is covered with one inch of water. Remove the meat from the water and you will have the proper amount of liquid for your brine.

To this liquid, add salt and dissolve thoroughly by stirring. Continue to add salt and stir until the solution will just float an egg. (The shell of the egg should barely break the surface of the solution.) Pack the meat carefully in the solution and place a clean plate over it. Weight the plate down with a clean stone or brick.

The dry brining method consists of rubbing all the dry salt or dry seasoned salt mixture possible into each individual piece of game. Pack the thoroughly salted pieces into a stone jar sufficiently large to hold all the salted pieces and still leave at least four inches at the top of the jar unfilled. When the salted pieces are carefully and closely packed in the jar, place a clean dinner plate over the meat and on top of it a clean stone or brick of sufficient weight to hold the meat pieces closely together. The meat will develop its own brine solution—enough to cover the meat.

The brining process should not last over three weeks—the time will depend on the size and thickness of the meat pieces used. Heavy pieces will require the full three weeks. Light strips, such as are used for jerky, will require no more than four or five days. For either the wet or dry process it is important to maintain a temperature of between 40° and 50°F. for brining.

Two methods of smoking game are normally used—the hot smoke method and the cold smoke. Temperature for hot smoking can vary from 140° to 170°F. The lower temperature will require more time to finish smoking but generally produces a better quality product. The cold smoking method uses temperatures between 90° and 120°F. This method requires a much longer smoking period—usually 48 hours—and it is very important that the same temperature be maintained throughout the period.

The advantage of hot smoking is that the process will both cook and cure the meat at the same time. But the keeping quality of the smoked meat is not as good as that produced by the cold smoking method. Hot smoking will require 4 to 6 hours, depending on the size and thickness of the pieces of meat to be processed.

The flavor of the finished meat is governed entirely by the type of wood used for creating the smoke. Dry hardwoods, often referred to as sweet woods, are necessary for creating the smoke if a palatable flavor is to be developed—such woods as hickory, apple, maple, buttonwood, mangrove and orange wood. Ground corncobs may also be used satisfactorily. Do not use any of the pine or conifer woods. They have a high resin content and are not suitable for use in smoking or smoke cooking. Also, green wood should not be used, for it will develop very unpleasant flavors and affect the keeping qualities of the finished product.

A number of aldehydes are found in wood smoke. Probably formaldehyde is the most prevalent, along with acetic acid. These two chemicals act as preservatives of flesh or tissue and at the same time increase the tensile strength of tissue and harden connective tissue. Therefore the longer the exposure of flesh to proper smoke, the more preservative will be absorbed—and the longer the keeping quality of the smoked flesh will be extended.

DRY CURE MIX

8 pounds pure pickling salt
2 pounds light brown sugar
2 ounces saltpeter

This amount of dry cure mix is sufficient for 100 pounds of meat. This mix can be used for most dry cure projects.

VENISON SMOKED SAUSAGE

2 parts lean venison
1 part prime beef chuck
Seasoning for each pound of meat:
2 teaspoons pure salt
1/4 teaspoon black pepper
1/8 teaspoon cayenne pepper
1/8 teaspoon mace
1/8 teaspoon coriander
1 clove garlic, crushed
1/16 teaspoon saltpeter
Sausage casings

Chop meat with a knife and sprinkle with seasoning mixture, mixing thoroughly. Grind meat twice in a meat grinder, using a medium blade. Put the ground meat in a stone crock or stainless-steel bowl and place in the refrigerator for 48 hours to permit seasonings to penetrate the meat. Stuff the mixture in large natural casings, using a sausage stuffer or sausage stuffing attachment for your grinder and making the sausages about 12 inches long. (Dried casings can be ordered from most any butcher. They come in large and small sizes and need only to be soaked in water before use.)

Make sure the casings are firmly stuffed. Hang the sausages in the smoker and smoke for 48 hours at 100°F. After the 48 hours of cool smoking, increase the temperature in the smoker to 150°F. and continue smoking for 24 hours. This final smoking period cooks the meat and adds to the keeping quality and flavor of the sausage.

DRIED VENISON

Cut off the rump portion of the hind leg of venison at the hip joint. Carefully separate the large muscles in the leg with your fingers and strip each muscle down to the gamble or first leg joint. Cut off the tendons from the joint, freeing each muscle. You will have pieces of meat 8 to 10 inches long—excellent venison for smoke drying.

Rub in dry cure mix, using as much cure as possible for each piece. Pack the pieces closely together in a stone jar large enough to hold all the meat. Sprinkle a light layer of curing mix over the last layer of meat. This will form a brine to cover the meat. Cure in this brine for 21 days. Remove the pieces and wash in clear water. Dry thoroughly. Put the individual pieces in stockinette or thin cheesecloth and tie with string. Place the pieces in the smoker on wire racks or tie to wood rods that will fit across your smoker.

Smoke for 48 hours at 110°F. Remove the pieces and hang to dry for 7 days. Place the pieces back in the smoker and continue smoking for 24 hours at 90°F. Remove the pieces and hang for 3 days to dry. Pieces may be double-wrapped in freezer paper and stored in the deep freeze.

157

Dried venison is excellent fare to take on a long hike or hunting trip. Sliced thin, you will find it very tasty and sustaining. It is also excellent when sliced very thin and prepared in a good cream sauce and served on toast points. It adds a great deal to the flavor of creamed fresh asparagus and makes a delicious one-dish meal.

Moose, elk, antelope and caribou meat can be treated in the same manner as venison. This curing method furnishes a means of using and keeping the meat and having delectable game to serve as well.

SMOKED JERKY

This meat can be prepared by cutting clear, lean pieces, free of any fat, into strips 1/2 inch thick—no thicker. The strips should be cut with the grain of the meat, not across the grain. Place the strips in a stone jar in layers one strip thick. Liberally apply the following curing mix to each layer. For each pound of meat strips, use:

2 tablespoons pure salt
1/4 teaspoon black pepper
1/8 teaspoon cayenne pepper
1 teaspoon garlic powder
1 tablespoon light brown sugar

If tough cuts are used for making the meat strips, meat tenderizer should be sprinkled over each layer.

Place the container of meat in the refrigerator for 24 hours. Remove the strips from the container; drain thoroughly and dry. Place the strips in the smoker, making sure that each strip is separate—not touching another strip. Smoke with a cool smoke of 90°F. for 2 to 3 days or until the strips are thoroughly dry. If the meat strips are not thoroughly dried, they can be finished in the oven at 150°—leave the oven door open for air circulation. When the strips are dry they are ready for eating or storing. They keep without refrigeration.

SMOKED WILD TURKEY OR PHEASANT

Place thoroughly dressed birds in a stone jar or large stone crock. Cover the birds with a curing solution made of 6 pounds of pure pickling salt, 3 pounds of light brown sugar and 3 ounces of saltpeter, dissolved in 4 1/2 gallons of clean water. Put a clean dinner plate over the birds and on the plate a clean rock large enough to hold the birds down in the curing solution. Put the jar in a cool place where the temperature can be held as close to 38°F. as possible. Remove the birds from the brine and repack once each week to make sure that the brine comes in contact with all parts of the birds. Cure the birds for 2 to 4 weeks, depending on the weight of the individual birds. The cured birds should be removed from the brine, thoroughly washed and hung up to dry. When the birds are dry, place or hang in the smoker and smoke at 100° to 110°F. for 3 to 4 days, smoking 8 to 10 hours each day. Remove the birds and hang to dry. When completely dry, double-wrap in freezer paper and store in the deep freeze. These birds must be cooked—either roasted or broiled—before eating.

SMOKE COOKING

Smoke cooking is essentially barbecuing, except that the cooking unit has a cover. This cover is 10 to 12 inches high over the cooking grill and it is equipped with vents that can be opened to allow a flow of air around the meat cooking on the grill. This type of cooker also has vents in the bottom below the fire grate that can be opened or closed to govern the draft or airflow into the cooker. These bottom and top vents are essential in a smoke cooking unit.

Other than this, a smoke cooking unit is the same as a barbecue grill. You use the same fuel for heat—charcoal briquets—and your fire grate can be raised or lowered as is necessary.

In smoke cooking the hot coals are placed in one end of the unit and the meat or fowl in the other end. Or the coals can be spread thinly around the outside edge of the fire grate and the meat placed in the center of the grill. In either situation a drip pan made of aluminum foil should be placed under the meat. The drip pan not only aids in keeping the cooker clean but also saves the fragrant and tasty juices from the meat to make excellent sauces and gravies.

To smoke cook, build your fire in the usual manner, then spread or place the coals as previously described. Place meat or fowl on the cooking grill and sprinkle a handful of wet hickory chips or sawdust over the coals. Close the cover on the cooker—and you are on your way to preparing a tasty meal.

You can determine the temperature inside the cooker by placing a meat roasting thermometer on the grill next to the meat. Some smoke cookers have a thermometer built into the cover for greater convenience in checking temperature.

Cooking with a covered cooker requires less fuel and a smaller fire, as there is very little heat loss. Also, the meat cooks on all exposed surfaces at the same time, due to the air circulation developed from the vents in the bottom and top.

With a covered cooker you avoid smoking and charring of meat from fat dripping on the fire. Instead you develop a very tantalizing flavor in the meat you are cooking by sprinkling wet hickory chips over the coals, or fresh herbs such as rosemary twigs, marjoram, thyme or mint. Dry bay leaves soaked in water until pliable, then chopped and sprinkled lightly over the coals, will also add a delectable flavor and bouquet to the meat or birds.

It is convenient to keep a 2-pound coffee can handy to the cooker with your wood chips or sawdust soaking in water. They should soak at least 45 minutes before being added to the fire. This permits you to have a supply of smoke fuel handy during the cooking period. Also, keep an additional supply of hot charcoal briquets available in an old metal pail when you are preparing a large roast or fowl. When the temperature in the cooker starts to fall, hot coals can be added to maintain correct cooking temperature. The hot coals can be placed in the cooker with barbecue tongs.

There are several makes of covered cookers with hinged tops that can be tipped back to permit getting to the meat, or the fire, to adjust its density. This type of cooker comes in many sizes and it is not difficult to find the size to fit your needs. Kettle-type cookers are also available in sizes from 15 inches in diameter to the large 26-inch size. Both kinds are excellent for smoke cooking.

Points to look for if you wish to buy a smoke cooker are:

1. A tight-fitting cover.

2. A damper control or vent in the cover.

3. Sufficient clearance between the grill and the cover top to permit cooking a large roast or a fowl such as a turkey. The distance between the grill and the top of the cover should be at least 10 inches.

4. A convenient and easy-to-use draft or air control on the bottom under the grate that holds the coals or fire.

5. The cooker should be of sufficient length to hold a large turkey or goose. This will assure you of ample room for anything you may wish to smoke cook.

SMOKE COOKED WILD GOOSE

6- to 8-pound dressed wild goose
2 cups pure salt
1 gallon clean water
3 large apples, diced
1 medium onion, chopped
1 cup diced celery
2 cups dry bread crumbs
1/4 pound bacon slices
2 tablespoons brown sugar
1 teaspoon ground sage
1/4 teaspoon ground thyme
1 teaspoon salt
1/4 teaspoon black pepper

Make a brine of the salt and the water in a stone jar or stainless-steel bowl large enough to hold the goose. Place the goose in the brine solution, making certain that it is entirely covered with brine. Leave in the brine for 10 hours in a cool place. Remove the goose from the brine and drain. Wipe it dry with a clean cloth or paper towel and rub with salt and pepper inside and out. Fry the bacon until crisp; remove from skillet and crumble. Add the apples, onion, celery and sugar to the bacon fat and sauté until the apples begin to soften. Add this to the bread crumbs along with the crumbled bacon, thyme and sage. Mix well; stuff and truss the goose.

Cook the goose on a rack over a foil pan at 325°F. in the smoke cooker. Cook 30 to 35 minutes per pound of the entire weight of the stuffed goose.

SMOKE COOKED QUAIL

Select two plump quail for each person. Make a stuffing of equal parts of chopped celery and onion. Stuff each bird and skewer. Put the quail breast on a rack over a pan, and place a piece of bacon over each bird. Season the birds with salt and pepper. Cook on a rack over a pan at 325°F. until tender. Use a medium amount of smoke while cooking. Baste the birds frequently with a solution made of 1 cup cooking sherry, 1 teaspoon dry mustard and 1/4 cup orange juice.

SMOKE COOKED WILD DUCK

Use one medium-sized duck per serving. Place one small onion and 1/2 of a medium navel orange in each duck. Rub the ducks well with salt and pepper. Place on a rack over a pan and cook at 325°F. 30 minutes for each pound of weight of the individual duck. Baste the ducks frequently with a mixture of 1 cup dry red wine, 1 tablespoon onion juice, 1/4 cup melted butter or margarine and 1 tablespoon Worcestershire sauce. After the basting solution has been used up, baste with the drippings from the pan. Use a medium amount of smoke from wet hickory chips for the baking period. Make a sauce or thin gravy from the pan drippings and pour over the ducks before serving. Discard the onion and half orange from the cavity of the duck before serving.

SMOKE COOKED PHEASANT

For one large pheasant, well cleaned and seasoned with salt and pepper inside and out, prepare a stuffing of 1/4 cup chopped onion, 1/4 cup chopped celery, 1/4 cup chopped black walnuts, 1 tablespoon brown sugar, 1 teaspoon grated orange rind, 1/4 teaspoon thyme, 1/4 teaspoon salt, 1/16 teaspoon black pepper, 2 tablespoons melted butter, 1 cup cooked wild rice or brown rice. (More rice can be added if necessary to fill the bird when stuffing it.) Fill the cavity of the bird well but do not pack.

Place the stuffed pheasant on a rack over a drip pan and cook at 325°F. in the smoke cooker in the area farthest from the hot coals. Cook for 2 hours or until fork-tender. Use medium smoke during the cooking period. Baste frequently with a mixture of 1 cup orange juice, 1/4 cup honey and 4 tablespoons melted butter or margarine. Baste with the pan drippings after the basting mixture is used up.

This recipe can be used for smoke cooked wild turkey as well. Increase the amounts of stuffing to fill the turkey and cook the turkey 35 minutes to the pound or until tender. Double the amounts of the ingredients for the basting liquid. This recipe will provide very juicy and tasty birds.

SMOKE COOKED LEG OF VENISON

Use a 5- or 6-pound rolled and boned leg of venison. The weight should be determined after the leg has been boned.

Make a marinade of 1/2 cup brown sugar, 1/2 cup salad oil, 1 teaspoon grated lemon peel, 1/4 cup lemon juice, 3 tablespoons tarragon vinegar, 1 teaspoon dry mustard, 1 teaspoon ground allspice and 1 teaspoon salt. Heat this mixture to boiling, reduce heat and simmer for 10 minutes; set aside and let cool. Place the rolled leg of venison in a stone crock or large glass bowl. Pour the marinade over the meat; cover and place in the refrigerator for 24 to 36 hours. The longer the meat is left in the marinade, the more pronounced the flavor will be when the meat is cooked.

Remove the venison from the marinade and insert a roast meat thermometer halfway into the thickest portion of the roast. Arrange the coals around the edge of the grate in the cooker. Place the roast on a rack on a drip pan and place on the center of the grill. Cook at 325°F. until the thermometer registers 165°F. At 30-minute intervals, sprinkle wet hickory chips over the coals. It will be necessary to add some hot coals to those in the cooker to maintain the 325° cooking temperature. Baste the roast with some of the marinade at 45-minute intervals.

THE SMOKEHOUSE

Several types and sizes of smokehouses or smokers are available to the sportsman interested in smoking his game.

It requires a little scrounging around to obtain the materials necessary to make a smoker of a size to fit your needs—and a little effort on your part to build a more or less permanent smoker.

If you want a rather large smoker, you can build a very efficient and inexpensive one by using the following specifications:

Make a smokehouse 3 feet square and 6 feet high out of 1 x 6 pine boards. Hang a door on one full side—that is, the door's dimensions would be 3 feet wide and 6 feet high. Fasten the door to one side of the smoker with two strap hinges. Install a screen door hook and screw eye on the opposite side of the door so that the door can be secured when it is closed. Leave the bottom of the smokehouse open. Make a false bottom for the inside of the smokehouse, supported by 1- x 2-inch strips nailed to the sides and back of the smokehouse, 12 inches up from the bottom of the smoker. The false bottom is made of 1/4-inch or 3/8-inch plywood or scrap boards nailed together.

Bore 1-inch holes, spaced 2 inches apart, all over the false bottom. Nail 1- x 2-inch pine cleats to the walls of the smoker 12 inches from the top to hold the first set of trays. Continue to make these tray supports at 12-inch intervals on down the inside of the smoker. The trays are made of 1- x 2-inch pine of the size to fit on the tray holders, then covered with 1/2-inch hardware cloth or 1-inch woven wire netting. Sticks or rods, to fit the width of the smoker over the cleats, can be used to hang meat, fowl or fish on for smoking.

Bore three 1-inch holes, 3 inches from the top of the smoker in the 3 sides of the smoker for ventilation and air circulation.

Place the smokehouse over a pit 2 feet square and 18 inches deep. A second pit, 3 feet square and 18 inches deep, should be made 4 feet from the pit under the smokehouse and the two pits connected with a trench 1 foot deep and 1 foot wide. The walls of the pits and the trench can be supported by pieces of tin or old corrugated metal roofing. Cover the 3-foot-square pit, which is your fire pit, and the trench, with tin or corrugated roofing metal. Pile 3 or 4 inches of dirt on the tin over the fire pit and trench. It is advisable to pile dirt 4 inches high around three sides of the smoker—leave the door free.

Your smoker is now ready for use. Build a small fire in the fire pit and let it burn down to a bed of coals. Add wood to the coals to maintain correct temperature in the smoker and proper smoke density.

A smaller smoker can be made from a 50-gallon metal drum. The drum must be clean to avoid undesirable odors and flavors, and it must have a removable top. The top of the drum can be cut out and a piece of plywood or tin large enough to cover the top can be used as a removable cover.

Take a 1/4-inch metal drill and put six equidistant holes through the drum, 3 inches from the bottom. Place 1-inch stove bolts through the holes and secure them inside the drum with nuts. Cut 3 holes, 1 1/4 inches in diameter, in the bottom of the drum. Place the holes in an 8-inch triangle in the center of the bottom. Cut a piece of 1/4-inch expanded metal to fit the inside of the drum and place it on the stove bolts at the bottom. This will be your fire grate.

Drill 6 1/4-inch holes, an equal distance apart, 6 inches from the top of the drum. Insert 1-inch stove bolts through the holes and secure them inside the drum with nuts. Cut another piece of 1/4-inch expanded metal to fit inside the drum and place it on the stove bolts. This serves as a rack for meat or fish when it is being smoked.

Place the drum on top of 4 bricks placed on the ground to allow free draft through the holes in the bottom of the drum. You can control the draft in the smoker by placing a small stick under the edge of the plywood cover. Now your drum-type smoker is ready for use.

An old discarded refrigerator can be made into a very efficient smokehouse quite easily. Cut or punch a few holes through the walls of the refrigerator, 1 inch in diameter and 3 inches from the top of the unit. Also, cut two or three holes in the bottom, depending on the size of the refrigerator. These holes should be 1 1/4 inches in diameter; they permit good air circulation through the smoker. The food racks in the refrigerator can be used to hold your meat, fowl or fish for smoking.

A small electric plate with a 3-way heat control—low, medium and high—is used for the heat supply. A two-pound coffee can is used for holding the wet wood chips or sawdust for the smoke supply. Fill the coffee can about one half full of wet chips or sawdust and set it on the hot plate. Turn on the hot plate to the necessary temperature and you are ready to start your meat smoking operation. The refrigerator door can be left a bit ajar for temperature control if necessary. Metal smokers hold the heat much better than smokers made of wood and it is necessary to watch the temperature inside the smoker carefully. Do not use a refrigerator with a plastic lining—it will develop very undesirable flavor and odor in the meat, fowl or fish.

A permanent and substantial smoker can be made of concrete blocks or bricks. Use the same general design and specifications given for the wooden smokehouse.

Hooded or kettle-type barbecue units can be used very satisfactorily for smoke curing small amounts of meat, fowl or fish. Keep the bed of coals at the edge of the cooker in one spot. Control the temperature in the cooker by adjusting the draft vents in the bottom and top. A very small amount of charcoal briquets is required for this method. Keep a supply of hot briquets available to be added to those in the cooker as needed. Wet wood, wood chips or sawdust is used for the smoke supply. Should they flame up, remove and add wet smoke material. The material removed can be resoaked and used again.

Electric smokers are available on the market for the sportsman who wishes to smoke small amounts of game or fish occasionally. A very efficient and well-constructed one is: Outers Hickory Smoker, made by Outers Laboratories, Inc., Onalaska, Wisconsin. These smokers are complete with an electric heating unit, a pan for wood chips or sawdust and necessary draft-control vents. They are large enough to hold a wild goose, a leg of venison or a pair of pheasants.

DO'S AND DON'TS OF SMOKING OR SMOKE COOKING

Never attempt to smoke meat, fowl or fish that has been frozen. Freezing ruptures the cells in the tissue of the flesh and the fluids will drain off after thawing. This leaves a very unsatisfactory product for curing or smoking.

Temperature inside the smoker is most important and must be constant throughout the smoking period in most instances. For the hot smoking method, temperature should be held between 160° and 170°F. For the cold smoking method temperature should be maintained at 90° to 100°F. A minimum or maximum amount of smoke has very little to do with the quality of the finished product.

The longer cold smoking method will produce a product that will keep much longer than the hot smoke method. Two weeks would be the maximum length of time to expect to keep the product from the hot smoke method. Cold smoked game or fish will keep fairly well for up to 60 days. However, it must be carefully wrapped in good freezer paper, then overwrapped with heavy foil. Keep the wrapped packages as nearly airtight as possible.

The fire for smoking should never flame. Keep the fire down to a bed of smoldering coals. Add wood as necessary, but do not add excessive amounts at one time. Keep the smoking wood wet and add a few pieces at a time—just enough to keep the bed of coals alive and a constant volume of sweet, fragrant smoke in the smoking unit.

The larger the smoker that you use, the larger the bed of smoldering coals that will be required to maintain a constant temperature.

THE HANDLING OF GAME

If it is warm enough for insects to be present, many hunters recommend placing game or game birds on top of pole at least sixteen feet in height or in a dead tree of the same height, when hanging meat in camp. Flies are rarely found at that distance above the ground and away from foliage. A rope pulled over the crotch of a dead tree or through a loop of rope fastened the proper distance above the ground can serve as a means of raising and lowering the meat as it is needed either for use or when more meat must be added. Game may be kept for some time if hung in the air with a netting to protect it from insects. It is best not to salt meat when hung this way, as the salt tends to draw out the juices.

Game may spoil more quickly or absorb bad flavor as a result of the food it has eaten just before being shot. Therefore, the time required for spoiling or the certainty of uniform flavor cannot always be depended upon, and individual animals or birds may vary widely in such respects.

Game birds or sections of game animals that have been badly shot up should be soaked for several hours in salt water before being used.

Once home, unless you are an accomplished butcher, it is wise to let someone who is make the individual cuts of your kill. An expert will do a quick, efficient job, and will give you the maximum amount of meat in the finest possible form.

On freezing game: When birds are to be frozen they should be cleaned and wrapped individually in plastic film, heavy-duty foil, or other moisture- and vapor-proof materials. The birds can then be handled as units at any time and removed from the freezing locker as desired.

Meat to be frozen should be cut into pieces, ready for cooking, and, like the birds, wrapped separately. If two or more pieces of meat are wrapped in one package, two sheets of plastic film or other moisture-and vapor-proof wrap should be placed between each of the cut surfaces— otherwise pieces will freeze into a solid block and cannot be separated until thawed out again. It is important to label each piece as it is wrapped for freezing in order to avoid confusion later on.

Meat frozen and maintained at 0°F. or colder will lose none of its fine

qualities over a period of 6 to 12 months, but the edible organs (heart, liver) should be used within the 6-month period.

Frozen meats can be cooked even when in a solidly frozen state. But for uniform cooking of the meat, it should be at least two-thirds thawed. In thawing, the rule is the slower the better, thus permitting the meat to retain the greatest amount of its moisture content. At room temperature, meat will usually thaw out at a rate of about 2 hours per pound. On the refrigerator shelf, 5 hours per pound should be allowed.

On preparing game for shipment: There is rarely any certainty, even during the coldest seasons, that game being shipped for any distance will not encounter a period during which it will be subject to temperatures high enough to cause spoilage. For that reason, game should be shipped in a frozen condition whenever possible. And every precaution should be taken to protect the meat against heat.

Birds should always be cleaned before shipment. When shipped in dry ice, they should be plucked or skinned, then frozen. If shipped with ordinary ice or without refrigeration, the feathers should be left on, or each bird should be wrapped individually in a moistureproof wrapper. Birds should never be frozen with the feathers on.

When your game is frozen and wrapped separately, it may be packed in a carton with dry ice and then wrapped with a moistureproof covering and sealed completely. The carton containing the dry ice and the game should be surrounded by a layer of crumpled newspaper or other insulating material and placed in a slightly larger carton to protect from heat.

The average loss of dry ice through evaporation while being shipped in cartons is about 20 percent in 24 hours. Allowance for such loss must be made when ordering ice for shipping. In addition, if possible, game should be frozen before packing in dry ice for shipment. If unfrozen game is

packed with the dry-ice refrigerant, it will freeze quickly, but the unfrozen meat will absorb a considerable quantity of the dry ice, leaving less for the job of cooling it on its journey. It is safer to be generous with dry ice rather than skimpy, as a little leftover at the end of a trip is far better than running short and subjecting the meat to heat damage.

Also order your dry ice in advance or at least make arrangements for its purchase when and where needed. A little investigation before the hunting starts may save a great deal of trouble or even some meat loss from spoilage. A few minutes spent on a phone call or a brief visit to the local freezing plant will pay dividends. The local express agent or air terminal may be able to advise you where to have your game frozen and packaged.

A 50-pound block of dry ice in a 100-pound carton will provide package allowance for more then 40 pounds of meat. Extra cartons, knocked down, may be ordered from the freezing plants together with the dry ice. To ship frozen game safely, allow 25 pounds of dry ice to 75 pounds of game to maintain frozen state for 5 days or longer.

From the Railway Express regulations: Meats, fresh or cured, dressed carcasses, or parts thereof, when not packed in outside containers must be covered with a heavy cloth or burlap, or enclosed in krinkled kraft paper bags and stockinets used in combination.

Carcasses from which hides have not been removed may be accepted without cloth or burlap covering. Cooked game, if shipped in sealed containers, may be safely shipped for considerable distances.

When shipping migratory birds, the number and species must be marked plainly on the outside of the package, together with the shipper's name and hunting license number. All game should be plainly labeled.

Check state laws, when shipping or storing game, to be certain that all necessary conditions are fulfilled, well in advance of a hunting trip.

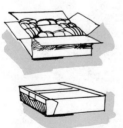
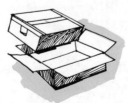

INDEX OF RECIPES

170

ABOUT THE EDITOR

L. W. "Bill" Johnson of Waupaca, Wisconsin, is called "The Hunter." He has earned the name and the reputation. Bill has hunted just about every game bird or animal you can think of throughout the United States. He has spent his entire adult life as a sales representative and professional shooter for Remington Arms Company. During World War II, he was a gunnery instructor.

Bill has toured the country as an exhibition shooter, and is well known as a true sportsman and a lover of the outdoors. For the past twelve years, Bill Johnson has conducted a weekly television program on WSAU-TV in Wausau, Wisconsin. The program, "The Hunter," is syndicated in various cities throughout the United States, and thousands of men, women and children viewers have been able to gather hunting information, hints and suggestions that Bill has spent a lifetime accumulating. He is an expert in the field.

The recipes here were gathered in response to a contest sponsored by Bill's television program. Only the most varied and interesting of the many recipes submitted were selected for this book.

Additional copies of this Wild Game Cookbook
can be obtained by sending $3.95 to
Cook Book
Box 432
Bridgeport, Connecticut 06601

I enclose $_____for_____copies of the book.

NAME_____

ADDRESS_____

CITY_____STATE_____ZIP_____

Additional copies of this Wild Game Cookbook
can be obtained by sending $3.95 to
Cook Book
Box 432
Bridgeport, Connecticut 06601

I enclose $_____for_____copies of the book.

NAME_____

ADDRESS_____

CITY_____STATE_____ZIP_____

Additional copies of this Wild Game Cookbook
can be obtained by sending $3.95 to
Cook Book
Box 432
Bridgeport, Connecticut 06601

I enclose $_____for_____copies of the book.

NAME_____

ADDRESS_____

CITY_____STATE_____ZIP_____